Power of Mantra

咒的魔力

by Sheng-yen Lu

Translated by Cheng Yew Chung

Foreword by Professor Tam Wai Lun

A US Daden Culture Publication

US Daden Culture LLC
3440 Foothill Blvd.
Oakland, CA 94601
U.S.A.
www.usdaden.com
us.daden.culture@gmail.com

Lu, Sheng-yen, 1945-
The Power of Mantra/by Sheng-yen Lu;
translated by Cheng Yew Chung;
edited by Jason Yu;
proofread by Renée Cordsen.

Library of Congress Control Number(PCN): 2010929499
ISBN-13: 978-0-9841561-1-5
ISBN-10: 0-9841561-1-9
1. True Buddha School. 2. Chinese-Tibetan Buddhism. I. Cheng Yew Chung 1965-

Cover design and layout by US Daden Culture Design Team
Photograph by Deanna Chan
Set in Minion Pro 12
US Daden books are printed on acid-free paper and meet the guidelines for the permanence and durability set by the Council of Library Resources.

Printed in U.S.A.

Special Acknowledgements

The True Buddha Translation Teams (TBTTs) would like to express the highest honor and deepest gratitude to Living Buddha Lian-sheng, Sheng-yen Lu, and Master Lianxiang for their continuing support and guidance on the translation effort. Without their compassion, wisdom, blessings, and encouragement, this project would not have reached fruition.

In addition, we would like to acknowledge the diligent work put forth by the following volunteers on this project: Cheng Yew Chung (translator), Jason Yu (editor), and Renée Cordsen (proofreader). We would like to thank these dedicated and selfless volunteers who have contributed their time and effort to promote the works of Living Buddha Lian-sheng, and to support the publications of the US Daden Culture.

We would also like to extend our sincere appreciation to all of the other volunteers who work behind the scenes, facilitating the translation process, and handling administrative responsibilities.

May all volunteers be blessed for their immeasurable merits; may all sentient beings benefit from the ocean of wisdom.

In my journey of practicing the teachings of the Buddha, I came across the teachings of the Yoga of One Taste. I entered the path of Mantrayana and realized that the Vajrayana teachings of mantras are able to fulfill all good wishes, and accomplish all great deeds.

Sheng-yen Lu

Table of Contents

Mantras are also known as dharanis - all encompassing and containing limitless dharma. Thus, we describe mantras as:

The true word
The illuminating spell
The heart of the Tathagata
The mani jewel

Sheng-yen Lu

Foreword

A majority of Han Chinese tend to describe themselves as either being non-religious or atheist. Only a relatively small percentage of them openly claim to be religious. However, a recent study of the religious experiences of the Han Chinese conducted between 2004 and 2006 has shown that 56.7% of people polled in China claimed to have had a spiritual experience that could not be ordinarily explained or controlled. These findings are comparable to some surveys conducted in the western countries by numerous scholars which consistently indicate that between one-third and one-half of the people interviewed have had a spiritual experience. On the other hand, Confucius taught us to respect the spirits but keep them at a distance. He asked, "While you are not able to serve men, how can you serve their spirits?" Also, "While you do not know life, how can you know about death?" Yet, many people say that it was precisely at a time when they were facing death that they began to realize the meaning of their life, and thus started to appreciate and understand life more. Furthermore, because the unseen and spiritual world remains the most bewitching and enchanting topic for many, it is too irresistible to be put at a distance.

Most of Grand Master Sheng-yen Lu's books, which now include over two hundred volumes, contain reports of many people's spiritual experiences and their encounters in the metaphysical world. This is one of the reasons why Grand Master Lu's books are so engaging and remain best-sellers, not only among his disciples but also in the Chinese reading world at large. Most of his books contain a collection of prose on a special theme, as well as modern poetry composed by Grand Master Lu. Both his beautifully written prose and poetry are regarded as exceptional pieces of literature and his books continue to remain as revered models of Chinese literature. Grand Master Lu's books are also assets for scholars examining the Chinese religious experience. His books are more than mere collections of reports and records of other people's religious experiences. Due to his own inspiring achievements in religious practice, Grand Master Lu's books are filled with religious insight and wisdom. They include valuable teachings on subjects such as Vajrayana Buddhism and Chan (Zen) Buddhism. Furthermore, he reveals many mysteries about the religious world.

Thanks to Grand Master Lu, we can now get a glimpse of an eternal world through his writing. His interpretations of people's religious experiences in his books have become a powerful, overwhelming and timely call for participation in inner cultivation. I would recommend Grand Master Lu's books, without reservation, to all students of religious studies and to those with an interest in religion.

This book, which contains fourteen captivating stories regarding the efficacy of religious incantations, is a classic example of the works produced by Grand Master Lu. Regrettably, Grand Master Lu's books have long been limited to the Chinese speaking world and I am overjoyed to learn that there is now a plan to systematically translate Grand Master Lu's books into English.

Kumārajīva (344 CE – 413 CE), one of the most prominent and well known translators of Chinese Buddhist scriptures, once said that the process of translation is similar to chewing rice and feeding it to people. Much of the original flavor is inevitably lost in the process. Coming from one of the greatest translators in the history of Chinese Buddhism, this gives us some idea about the many challenges involved in translating sacred texts. Kumārajīva, however, never stopped translating and his translations of the *Heart Sutra, Lotus Sutra* and *Diamond Sutra*, for instance, remain the standard and most widely-read versions of the Chinese Buddhist texts. As Grand Master Lu's books' are considered the sacred texts of True Buddha School, the translation of these important works is a challenging, admirable and rewarding endeavor. I would like to offer my special thanks to the translation teams for a job well done!

February 8, 2010
Hong Kong

PROFESSOR TAM WAI LUN
Department of Cultural and Religious Studies
The Chinese University of Hong Kong

The water ghost realized an invisible energy field was covering the four corners of the bed, shielding me like a net of light. The bed itself was transformed into a lotus flower. I was transformed into a vajra. A net of light encircled me. The water ghost knew he had met his match and knelt down with his palms together.

Sheng-yen Lu

1 Curing a Fever with Mantra

I will begin with a story that happened years ago.

One day, a student of mine named Chen Jian hurried to my house and requested an immediate consultation.

"What's the matter?" I asked.

"Somebody really needs help!"

"Who?"

"My neighbor."

"Your next door neighbor?" I was amused, "What has that got to do with you?"

In a serious manner, Chen Jian replied, "Grand Master! I often tell my neighbors of your great merits and deeds. I tell them about your great dharma power and how you have resolved many problems for others. 'If there is a problem, just go to Living Buddha Lian-sheng and all will be resolved.' Today, my neighbor's only son came down with a fever and it just won't go away. I came on his behalf to seek your help."

"To treat a fever, they should see a doctor!" I said.

"They have consulted doctors and the child has taken the medicine, but the fever remains!"

"What about consulting a barefoot doctor or taking some Chinese herbal medicine?" I added.

"They consulted all kinds of doctors, but none could cure the child's fever. That's why I seek your help. Grand Master is a master of talismans and mantras."

"Haha, I am a talisman master!"

We hurried to the home of Chen Jian's neighbor. On arrival, I saw two encephalitis ghosts about to enter the house. I told the two ghosts, "Wait. Let me enter first." I pushed the two ghosts aside and they fell flat to the ground. They were fuming and screaming.

"Grand Master, who were you talking to earlier?" Chen Jian asked.

"To the air," I replied.

Once in the house, I met up with the house owners, Mr. and Mrs. Deng, whose son's fever had persisted for several days. They looked worried and asked if I could save their son.

"Your son has encephalitis, an inflammation of the brain," I said.

The couple's eyes were wide open upon hearing my diagnosis and exclaimed, "That's exactly what the doctor suspected and told us, and you knew it right away! Please help him, he's our only son!"

"You're fortunate to have met me. If not, your son would be doomed."

"How are you going to save him?" the couple asked.

"I'll use a mantra."

"A mantra can cure a fever?" the couple was astonished.

"Just watch."

I formed the Precious Hand Mudra with my right hand (the ring finger is extended and slightly bent, while the thumb presses over the rest of the folded fingers), and formed the Vajra Fist Mudra with my left hand (the middle finger, ring finger and little finger are folded over the thumb, while the index finger is lowered to touch the back of the thumb). I placed my left hand at my waist. Using the Precious Hand Mudra, I wrote the [Sanskrit] seed syllable VAM on the child's forehead and chanted, "VAM VAM VAM." Afterwards, I stomped on the floor three times with my left foot.

I said, "OK! The fever will soon subside."

"You mean the fever will go away just like that?" the couple uttered in disbelief.

What happened then was, not even two minutes later, the fever dropped and everything became normal. Once the fever went away, the child felt great, as if he was never sick.

The child recalled, "As I was feeling sick and drowsy, I saw a flaming cart coming towards me. Behind me was another cart in flames, blocking my retreat. I was doomed to die in that fire. All of a sudden, a man appeared in the sky and chanted some kind of mantra. He was riding on a cloud and his finger pointed right at me. With this, a downpour of rain came and extinguished the fire. I was saved and then woke up."

"Do you recognize the man in the sky?"

"Sure!" the boy exclaimed.

He pointed his finger at me and said, "That's him!"

"Wow!" shouted Chen Jian.

I nodded. The couple was definitely convinced.

Thus:

If you chant a mantra diligently
With persistence and practice you will quickly advance
Once you gain response by chanting a mantra
All of heavens will extend their help to you
In time, you will attain immortality

What exactly is a mantra? How can a mantra cure a fever? A practitioner chants a mantra and summons the Heavenly Water Deity to descend. Among mantras, the seed syllable VAM means water. You fight fire with water, and then the fire is subdued and the fever goes away. It is that simple.

Mantras are also known as dharanis - all encompassing and containing limitless dharma. Thus, we describe mantras as:

- The true word
- The illuminating spell
- The heart of the Tathagata
- The mani jewel

I feel that our time on earth is very short and the time that we can really use is scarce. If you spend all your time pursuing fame and wealth, you should know that you can lose it all in one moment.

I have always felt that the most important matter in life is the subject of life and death. To truly understand and transcend life and death by becoming enlightened is indeed the most meaningful thing.

When I practice the teachings of the Buddha, I realize the dharma is simply supreme and remarkable. There are many gems within the teachings, such as:

- The True Nature of Emptiness
- The Prajna Wisdom
- The Right View of the Middle Path
- The Consciousness-only Manifestation
- The Yoga of One Taste

I have seen many people who practice Zen Buddhism, and many who embrace the Pure Land School's chanting of the Buddha's name and sutras. There are those who follow the laws and rules of the Buddhist teachings, such as those who embrace the Vinaya School. There are other sects and schools that enable one to attain peace and happiness. Upon death, an individual ascends to the Pure Land, leaves the cycle of reincarnation, realizes his true self and gains enlightenment. He then roams freely in this world and beyond.

In my journey of practicing the teachings of the Buddha, I came across the teachings of the Yoga of One Taste. I entered the path of Mantrayana and realized that the Vajrayana teachings of mantras are able to fulfill all good wishes, and accomplish all great deeds. The Vajrayana teachings can eradicate disasters, enhance fortune, improve relationships and subdue all evils. The Vajrayana teachings can attract fortune and extend longevity and happiness within the family. You can certainly attain buddhahood through the teachings.

The buddhas and bodhisattvas have great compassion for all sentient beings and to liberate them from suffering, they utter dharanis [which are long mantras]. When we recite these mantras, they help us find peace and joy, receive great benefits, ease our lives and bring good fortune. They can even help eradicate our karmic hindrances within this lifetime and deliver us to the Pure Land.

Guru Tsongkhapa, the founder of the Gelug tradition of Tibetan Buddhism, once said, "To chant a buddha's name is to reflect his identity. To chant a mantra is to touch a buddha's heart."

In the book *The Essence of Vajrayana*, it is written, "If you combine the practice of chanting the Buddha's name and the chanting of mantra, your merit is as wide as the seas of Mount Sumeru. If you chant only the Buddha's name and not the mantra, your merit is but the size of Gandhamadana, the incense mountain located near Lake Anavatapta in Tibet."

In another book titled *As Small as Lake Anavatapta*, it is written, "The Pure Land School reaches to all levels of sentient beings. However, not everyone makes it to the highest of the nine stages of birth in the Pure Land. If an individual follows the practice of Vajrayana, he will gain access to the Pure Lands of the Ten Directions. He will definitely be successful in attaining the highest level of existence in the Pure Land."

Living Buddha Lian-sheng, Sheng-yen Lu says, "By chanting the buddha's name, one creates rapport with the buddha's identity. By chanting the mantra, one gains access to the buddha's heart. If you practice chanting both, you correspond with the outer and inner aspects of the Buddha, and this is most complete."

Thus:

> **Attain the clarity of mind through chanting the buddha's name**
> **Connect with the heart of the Tathagata through chanting mantras**
> **Realize the ultimate bliss as one complete reality**
> **You hear the cries of the world through one mantra**

Contact Address:
Sheng-yen Lu
17102 NE 40th Ct.
Redmond, WA 98052
U.S.A.

2 Eradicating All Disasters

A man by the name of Shen Ding was a chief engineer on a deep sea fishing ship.

When he was in Hong Kong, a friend invited him to consult a very famous fortune-teller, who was skilled in the art of Chinese divination known as "Tie Ban Shen Shu."

This form of Chinese divination requires the information of one's birth date and time, right down to the exact minute of birth. If the information is accurate, the divination will reveal the most accurate details of one's life.

Shen Ding felt that this art of divination, which was first revealed by Shao Kangjie in ancient China, was indeed remarkably accurate.

The fortune-teller revealed Shen Ding's destiny. He stated that his father was born in the year of the dragon and his mother was born in the year of the monkey. The information was correct.

He also mentioned that Shen Ding had three elder brothers and one younger sister. This was also correct.

The fortune-teller revealed that Shen Ding's mother passed away when he was ten years old. This astonished Shen Ding because what he said was indeed true. His mother died of a certain illness when he was only ten.

The fortune-teller proceeded to describe Shen Ding's destiny:

Shen Ding's livelihood was connected with water (Shen Ding worked on a deep sea fishing ship).

When he turned thirty, he met a friend by the last name Xie and lost his money (at age thirty, a friend with the last name Xie borrowed seven hundred thousand Taiwanese dollars and then disappeared).

The divination also revealed that Shen Ding had a girlfriend with the last name Zhang and disclosed exactly how much he earned per month. This was most astonishing to Shen Ding, leaving him dumbfounded.

Finally, when the fortune-teller came to Shen Ding's life span, he fell silent.

Shen Ding was eager to know how long he was going to live.

"It is best that you do not know," replied the fortune-teller.

"Whether my life will be long or short is not important. I can handle it," Shen Ding said.

The fortune-teller insisted on keeping quiet about his time left on earth.

Shen Ding exploded and said, "Look! I told you I can take it. People live and die. Whether life is long or short, so be it. Having a long life may not be a good thing. I want to find out how long I am going to live. If you don't tell me, I'm not going to leave."

The fortune-teller was in a very difficult position, as Shen Ding demanded to know.

Finally, the fortune-teller picked up one of the books on divination, flipped to the respective page and showed Shen Ding what was written on it. The respective sentence stated, "You will die at age thirty seven."

"Thirty seven! Thirty seven!" Shen Ding was shocked to learn of his life span.

Damn! Shen Ding was thirty five and that meant another two years before he left the world for good. Judging from the accuracy of this fortune-teller, it seemed that his life would surely come to an end at that age. Shen Ding claimed that he did not mind, but his heart was pounding.

Shen Ding asked, "Is there a way to change it?"

"Everything is destined by divine will. You can change your destiny through gathering good merits. I can't help you."

"Doing good deeds?"

"Yes."

"Just like *Liao Fan's Four Essays on Karma*," Shen Ding said. He has read that book.

"Pretty much," said the fortune-teller.

"But are two years enough time to change my destiny?" asked a worried Shen Ding.

The fortune-teller smiled and refused to comment.

"Is there someone on earth who can help change my destiny?"

The fortune-teller said, "To my knowledge, this form of divination is extremely accurate. I am aware that one can change his destiny, but this is rarely possible. There is one person you can talk to and see if he can help you."

"Which person?"

"Living Buddha Lian-sheng, Sheng-yen Lu."

"Can he really change my destiny?"

"Why not give it a try?"

* * *

When Shen Ding came to me, he did not mention his consultation with the fortune-teller in Hong Kong. He only forwarded a note stating that he wanted to know how long he had to live.

I said to him, "I never do readings to determine the length of one's life."

"Why not? Isn't it possible that we can find out about our marriage, our wealth, our children, and our state of prosperity?"

"Well, you're right in a way. But if I determine your life span and it turns out to be a short life, you'll become frightened. To avoid unnecessary complications, I avoid going into it."

"Can you make an exception?" Shen Ding requested.

"No," I replied.

"Alright. Any age is a two-digit number. How about you just tell me the last digit of the age and not the first digit. Is that OK?"

I gave it some thought and felt that it was fair enough. The last digit would not give away the length of a person's life span, and was thus meaningless. However, I was unclear why Shen Ding requested to know the last digit of his age of death.

I consulted the divination and wrote down the number seven.

Shen Ding looked at the number and said, "Seven. That's precisely the number!"

Shen Ding then revealed he had consulted a fortune-teller in Hong Kong who had told him that he would live to the age of thirty-seven. He wanted to know how he could reverse this situation and if I could change his fate.

I told him, "I can give it a try."

I went into deep meditation.

In my meditation, I saw a figure of Guanyin Bodhisattva dressed in a white robe, carrying a vial of elixir and a stalk of willow leaves in her hands. She appeared noble and at ease with herself. The Bodhisattva told me, "All you have to do is to tell Shen Ding to chant the mantra of the White Robed Guanyin Bodhisattva twenty times per day, and I will protect him. You don't have to teach him how to recite it because he already knows how."

I came out of my meditation and said to Shen Ding, "You know how to chant a mantra."

"Nonsense!" Shen Ding denied.

"But the Bodhisattva says you do."

"The Bodhisattva must be joking! I have never chanted any mantra in my entire life."

"The White Robed Guanyin told me that you know how to chant her mantra."

"Ah!" Shen Ding was taken aback. He then related this story to me.

About ten years ago, Shen Ding's aunt passed away. Before she died, she gave him a painting of a portrait of the White Robed Guanyin. The mantra of this Bodhisattva was written alongside the painting. His aunt had meticulously taught Shen Ding every word of this mantra. He had indeed chanted this mantra, and his pronunciation of it was very accurate. His aunt told him that the painting with the mantra has been kept and worshipped over a long period of time. The mantra was to be recited over the course of one's lifetime, and could not be neglected. According to his aunt, the mantra was very powerful.

Shen Ding kept this painting properly and recited the mantra of the White Robed Guanyin for a short period. After his aunt passed away, he put the painting away and never brought it out. He had since stopped chanting the mantra.

I told Shen Ding, "Hang up the painting of the Bodhisattva immediately."

"Yes," Shen Ding answered.

"Recite this mantra of the White Robed Guanyin twenty times a day."

"Yes."

"Do you want me to teach you how to recite it?"

"There's no need. I still remember how to chant this mantra."

Surprisingly, Shen Ding was able to write down this mantra:

The Mantra of the White Robed Guanyin

Namo the All Compassionate and All Merciful Guanyin Bodhisattva Mahasattva (three times)**.**

Namo Buddha ye.

Namo Dharma ye.
Namo Sangha ye.
Namo Guanyin Bodhisattva, the Great Compassionate One.
[transliteration:] Da-die-duo, om, ga-luo-fa-duo, ga-luo-fa-duo, ga-he-fa-duo, luo-ga-fa-duo, luo-ga-fa-duo, so-ha
[Sanskrit: TADYATA OM GARAVATA GARAVATA GAHAVATA RAGAVATA RAGAVATA SVAHA].
Summon the gods in the heavens,
Summon the gods on earth,
Deliver us from all disasters.
Remove us from all evils.
Reduce all disasters to nothingness.
Namo Maha Prajna Paramita.

When Shen Ding returned home, he hung his painting of the Bodhisattva on the wall and worshipped it with much reverence. In preparation for his daily chanting, he would clean his hands, light incense and prostrate before the image of the Bodhisattva before chanting the mantra. After completing his chanting, he would recite the dedication verse:

May karmic hindrances and defilements be removed
May wisdom and true realization be attained
May all transgressions be eradicated completely
May I follow the path of a bodhisattva life after life

Shen Ding added, "Guanyin Bodhisattva, please protect me when I am in danger, and grant me longevity."

At home, he could keep to the routine of his practice. But Shen Ding was, after all, a traveling chief engineer with his deep sea fishing ship. He spent most of his time away from home. Nonetheless, he taped a photo of the White Robed Guanyin at a corner of his cabin onboard his ship. He did not stop his daily practice.

His friends sneered at him and thought he was superstitious, crazy, and had lost his mind, but Shen Ding ignored them.

Besides chanting the mantra, Shen Ding committed himself to doing charity work whenever possible.

* * *

When he was thirty-seven, Shen Ding's fishing ship anchored at Hawaii before sailing to Guam the following day. That very night, Shen Ding had a bad stomach ache and was in great pain.

After being rushed to the emergency room in the hospital, he was diagnosed with acute appendicitis and needed an operation right away. Under these circumstances, Shen Ding had to stay behind at the Hawaiian hospital.

However, the ship was scheduled to leave for Guam and could not wait for him. Thus the ship sailed on without Shen Ding and arranged to meet with him again after his surgery.

Sadly, the ship sank on its journey to Guam when it encountered a heavy storm. None of the crew survived the tragedy. The ship and crew sank without a trace. Despite rescue attempts from the shipping company to search the area with helicopters and other rescue ships, they could not locate the missing crew. It was as if they had all vanished into thin air.

Because his acute appendicitis required him to stay behind in Hawaii for surgery, Shen Ding became the sole survivor of this tragedy.

Shen Ding later returned to Hong Kong and met up with the fortune-teller.

He told the fortune-teller, "Your divination was not accurate!"

The fortune-teller was astonished and exclaimed, "What happened?"

"I chanted the mantra of the White Robed Guanyin, that's all!"

The fortune-teller marveled and said, "The mantra has such miraculous power. It is indeed rare. I would like to chant it too."

Since then, Shen Ding has developed a deep faith in the White Robed Guanyin, and knew that the compassionate Bodhisattva would certainly answer the cries of all. He knew he must trust the Bodhisattva completely and be sincere; only then could a miracle be evoked. Shen Ding later took refuge in True Buddha School.

I taught Shen Ding how to practice the Four Preliminary Practices and the Guru Yoga. Eventually, he regarded the White Robed Guanyin as his personal deity [Tibetan: yidam] during his cultivation.

Shen Ding felt sorry for the shipmates and crew who had perished in the ocean. He decided to chant the mantra of the White Robed Guanyin one hundred two thousand times. He would then dedicate the merits of the mantra chanting to their spirits.

After the dedication of merits, Shen Ding had a dream. He dreamed of sailing in the ocean and his ship being surrounded by about fifty white birds. The circling birds seemed to come to say thank you to Shen Ding, and one by one, they each flew away. When he woke up from his dream, he realized that the spirits of his friends had all been liberated by the White Robed Guanyin and had left the sea of suffering.

Thus:

From dust to dawn he chants diligently
The White Robed Guanyin enters his dream frequently
The shipmates of the boat have been delivered
Bonded by a great affinity of old friendship

3 Grandfather's Prayer Beads

In the past, whenever I read the feng shui of a person's home, I observed both the visible and invisible worlds. The invisible world refers to the realm of spirits.

I will divulge a great secret.

I was once invited to do a feng shui consultation for a certain wealthy and powerful family in Kaohsiung, Taiwan. Once I entered the house, I saw many "ghosts of poverty" occupying the place. These ghosts had all come to collect debts [from the owner]. I instantly knew that this prestigious person would soon lose his wealth altogether. Indeed, soon afterwards, his business failed miserably.

On another occasion, I visited the home of a poor man in a village to read the feng shui of his house. His house was in the typical style of a Chinese village courtyard. I saw lots of spirits, like an army of ants, carrying sacks of golden sand on their backs marching to his house. One by one they entered his house to deliver the golden sand. I knew right away that the family would soon possess great wealth. Eventually, his name became well known and he held a position in government. His wealth increased astronomically and he became the country's wealthiest man.

These are my experiences of reading feng shui:

If "ghosts of poverty" demanding payment surround the individual, he is doomed to be a failure in life. If wealth deities surround the individual, he is destined to prosper. Thus, the invisible hand of spirits affects everything.

I once went to a night market in front of a temple for a late-night snack. In front of the temple was an empty lot with a small food vendor. The vendor only sold four items, which were herbal soup, noodles, rice flour rolls, and boiled vegetables.

There were many tables around the vendor and they were all occupied with customers who were eager to taste the food. It was very similar to ants going after cookies. I opened my divine eye to examine the man running the vendor, and what I witnessed was frightening. The open field was filled with more than a hundred patrons visiting the vendor, and an equal number of spirits roaming the area. These spirits had swayed the customers to patronize this vendor. When the spirits lured someone in, the person couldn't help but go in.

The vendor was famous for its herbal soup, and it was delicious. Every night, customers flowed in and out like an ocean tide. His business was so good that the money flowed in like running tap water. Some people said that the vendor owner laughed with delight while counting his money at home. Others said that the vendor owner owned a few apartments and his wealth was measured in the hundreds of millions.

I paid close attention to the vendor owner's facial features. I observed that his face was dark and gloomy, with a sunken nose, tiny mouth, small eyes and hardly any flesh on his face. He certainly did not look like he was a man of great wealth but instead resembled an old homeless man.

I felt there was nothing remarkable about this old man, but the fact that he was so prosperous was really strange! Besides being rich, he had so many spirits helping lure customers to his vendor. The spirits also attended to the customers and cleaned up their tables - this was quite perplexing.

I suspected that the old man learned how to use spirits to help him. However, upon closer observation, although he looked unpleasant, he did not have any negative energy lingering around his body.

From a distance, I looked at the vendor and the piece of land it was on and observed some glowing beams of red light emerging from the ground, and a red cloud quietly covered the area. This might have explained why the vendor was so prosperous. Perhaps it was due to the auspicious feng shui of the location. The other vendors did not enjoy the same kind of customer traffic that this vendor did. They were barely making ends meet. This was indeed interesting.

* * *

One day, a certain individual came to seek my consultation. He wanted to find a name for his grandson, and when I looked at him, I realized he was the same old man who ran the vendor.

I said to him, "Your business is doing very well!"

"It's nothing, nothing at all," the old man said modestly.

"How come your business is doing so well?" I asked curiously.

"Luck is on my side," the old man grinned, exposing his two rows of black teeth.

"I believe there is more than just luck," I said.

"Would you do a divination for me?" he requested.

The old man wrote down his name, birthday and address.

I made a quick spiritual observation and sensed the sound of a mantra filling the atmosphere, accompanied by the scent of sandalwood. I also saw circles of light radiating and within each circle stood a fortune deity. This was most astonishing.

"Do you know how to recite any mantras?" I asked.

"Nope!" Pan Ji, the old man, replied.

"I heard the sound of a mantra and smelled the scent of sandalwood. I saw fortune deities by your side."

"Impossible!"

I had helped many in my consultations and had a good track record of accuracy. It was rare to hear someone remark "impossible." Rather, it was impossible for my divine eye and divine ear to make a wrong observation. If there was ever any mistake in my observation, I was always able to pinpoint the cause of it.

"Does anyone at your home know how to chant any mantras?" I asked him.

"Neither my wife nor my kids know how to chant any mantras," Pan Ji replied.

"Do any of your other relatives know how to chant any mantras?" I asked.

"Do the deceased count?"

"Yes," I replied.

Pan Ji proceeded to tell me, "In my family, only my grandfather, Pan Li, knew how to chant a mantra. He held great respect for the God of Fortune and Virtue, and had built a temple for him. Subsequently, He also became the temple's guardian. Once, a monk gave my grandfather a string of prayer beads and taught him how to chant the Earth Deity Mantra. My grandfather recited the mantra his entire life using the prayer beads. He chanted with the prayer beads so much that it eventually turned black and became shiny."

"Where are the prayer beads now?" I believed I had found the answer.

"My grandfather passed them down to my father, and my father gave it to me, but I don't know where I put them. I think I'll ask my wife to help me find them."

Pan Ji returned home and asked his wife about the prayer beads. She told him, "They are tucked away inside a hidden crack at your vendor. Nobody knows about it."

Pan Ji searched for and found them in the vendor. He then took the darkened prayer beads and showed them to me. He did not know the value of the prayer beads.

I told Pan Ji, "Your grandfather, Pan Li, received protection from the Earth Deity. This is the result of reciting the Earth Deity Mantra, showing the Earth Deity respect, visualizing the Earth Deity and praising the Earth Deity."

The Earth Deity Mantra is as follows:

> **[transliteration:] Namo san-man-doh, moo-toh-nam, om, doo-loo-doo-loo, dei-wei, so-ha**
> **[Sanskrit: NAMO SAMANTA BUDDHANAM OM DURU DURU DEVI SVAHA].**

The Earth Deity Mantra is usually chanted before reciting a sutra. This is to summon the Earth Deities of the Four Directions to guard over you while you recite sutras.

Pan Li spent his entire life reciting this mantra. His sincerity moved the Earth Deities to protect him. This mantra is neither from the buddhas, bodhisattvas nor the vajra protectors. It is not a major mantra, yet it should not be underestimated as it contains amazing power.

If anyone is troubled by spiritual entities and recites this mantra, the spirits will retreat and respect you.

If anyone contracts a serious illness and recites this mantra, the illness will vanish. All pain will disappear and one's good health will return.

In the past, I had taught people how to chant this mantra as it is especially helpful for curing several forms of dermatitis, such as athlete's foot, chronic dermatitis, discoid eczema, etc. By chanting the mantra, those who have skin-related illnesses should be cured because the Earth Deity devours the bacteria on the skin.

If one recites this mantra diligently, abides by the Five Precepts and carries out the Ten Good Deeds, then one will not fall into the three lower realms and hell. In fact, one will be reborn in the heavenly realms and enjoy utmost bliss and joy. The Earth Deity Mantra is also extremely effective in terms of accumulating wealth because the Earth Deities and their spiritual attendants will help those who recite the mantra to receive measureless fortune.

Pan Li devoted his life to chanting this mantra and achieved great results with it. The prayer beads were passed down from grandfather to father, then from father to son, and the blessings were passed down as well. This was simply incredible.

Thus, I wrote a verse:

Filled with joy while reciting the Buddha's name and mantra
Now there is lineage in the Saha world
Continue to recite sincerely and respectfully
The blessing of deities and spirits will be with one perpetually

There is another story related to the Earth Deity Mantra.

There was a period when an epidemic swept through Taiwan and many livestock were killed. I observed many plague ghosts roaming in the wild and biting the animals to death. Owners of many farms approached me for help.

I studied the constellations and noted that the Five Plague Deities had descended from the southeastern area of the sky. This meant that an epidemic would sweep across the region, resulting in the deaths of many chickens, ducks, cattle, sheep and pigs.

I was worried, so I approached Cheng Huang, the City God, for help. He said, "This is fate, it has nothing to do with me!"

"Even if it is the will of the heavens, I cannot just watch people suffer."

"Don't interfere. People's hearts are too corrupted."

"It's hard for me to be at peace if I don't try to help them!" I said.

Cheng Huang said to me, "You, Sheng-yen Lu, try to help people every day, but their suffering is due to their own actions. One day, if someone hurts you, I wonder if anyone will save you."

I answered, "If someone hurts me, that's my own karma - but looking at all these livestock suffering, I really feel for them in my heart."

Cheng Huang then taught me a solution.

Take four sticks of bamboo and chip away the green outer layer. Each stick must be one foot six inches long. On an Accomplishment Day of the lunar calendar, chop the bamboo sticks. On each stick, inscribe the letters of the Earth Deity Mantra in either Chinese or Sanskrit.

In the afternoon of a lunar Removal Day, consecrate the bamboo sticks. Recite the Earth Deity Mantra one hundred and eight times for each stick. The more you recite the better. On a lunar Stability Day, hammer the bamboo sticks into the four corners of the ground of the respective farm.

When this is completed, a plague will not touch the respective farm. I taught this method to the farm owners and it worked! Each farm that was lined with the mantra-empowered bamboo sticks was protected from the plague. Not even one livestock animal died.

However, many other farmers were unaware of this method and during that year when the epidemic occurred, a lot of livestock died. There was hardly enough time to bury every dead chicken and cattle, and the carcasses piled up high like a hill.

One farm owner relayed this incident to me.

One night, he overheard a conversation that took place outside his farm. However, it was not human beings but plague ghosts who were talking. A large number of them arrived outside the farm.

One ghost exclaimed, "An aura produced by a certain mantra surrounds this farm. We cannot enter."

"What mantra?" another asked.

"The Earth Deity Mantra."

"That mantra is no big deal. It cannot stop us. Let's go!"

"No way!"

"Why not?"

"The Earth Deity is, after all, a virtuous god."

"We have our orders by heavenly decree!" the ghost shouted.

"But this mantra is empowered by Living Buddha Lian-sheng, Sheng-yen Lu himself."

"Really!"

The ghosts fell silent. One of them suggested, "Let's leave this place! We can feed ourselves elsewhere. Besides the small Earth Deity Mantra, there's also the Buddha's edict. It's better to leave it alone."

Thus, this bunch of ghosts left the farm.

Let me share this with you. Many wealthy men owe their riches to the help of spirits. Many disasters are the result of mischief from spirits. All of these incidents are caused by spiritual entities.

Confucius once said, "Respect the spiritual world but keep your distance." This means that the spiritual world does exist, but keep your interactions with them to a minimum.

In the Bible, Jesus once expelled spirits and exorcised demons. In the Catholic's instruction for the Exorcistate, the third of the Minor Orders, it outlines the rite of exorcism. The seventy-five-year-old Father Amorth is himself a famous Catholic exorcism priest!

The invisible spirits are worthy of our attention!

4 The Vajra Teeth

When I was young, my mother, Lu Yunu, told me a story. Once, there was an old woman who had lost all of her teeth due to her old age. It was very difficult for her to eat anything without her teeth. She could not eat solid food, so she could only eat liquid food.

The old woman's daughter-in-law was very filial and caring and always served her mother-in-law with the greatest care. She was sad to see how the old woman struggled with food, but she did not have a solution for the problem.

The daughter-in-law gave birth to a boy one day and she breast-fed the baby. Her breast milk was very nutritious and filling. After feeding the baby, she continued to produce milk. The daughter-in-law thought of her mother-in-law and instinctively took the old lady into her arms and breast-fed her. Her mother-in-law was old and was so light that it felt like she was cradling a small child in her arms.

The old woman had no teeth and could only drink her liquid food, so she suckled on her daughter-in-law's milk and had a full meal.

The baby grew well and the old woman's mental acuity and health greatly improved after the breast-feeding. The baby's teeth began to come through, but the most amazing thing was the fact that the old woman's gums began to harden. Eventually she grew thirty-eight new teeth! Don't you think this is amazing?

When I first heard this story, I thought it was simply impossible. My mother had mentioned that:

1. Breast milk is more nutritious than any manufactured milk products.
2. Breast milk is rich in calcium.
3. The filial act of the daughter-in-law moved the heavens.

This was a rather familiar story. Later in life, a traditional Chinese doctor told me that human breast milk is very nutritious. Babies that feed on their mother's milk usually do not fall sick very easily, and they have a naturally strong immune system.

The doctor told me that breast milk was known as "celestial wine" in traditional Chinese medicine:

Celestial wine,
Celestial wine,
Here on earth you will readily find.

* * *

My life was touched by the spiritual realm and thereafter I began my mission to help and liberate sentient beings in every way possible. Throughout all of this, I have encountered the strangest things and some of these encounters were simply magical and beyond comprehension. One of them even involved teeth!

There was a Buddhist by the name of Jiang Wei who came to me for a consultation.

"What would you like to find out?" I asked.

He kept silent. Instead he opened his mouth to show me his teeth.

I noticed a missing front tooth in the upper row of his teeth and it was obvious to anyone there was a gap there.

Jiang Wei said, "I lost this front tooth naturally. It just loosened up and dropped off. Now I am stuck with this gap. First of all, it looks ugly. Second, there's a lisp whenever I talk. Next, my saliva shoots out uncontrollably and lastly, according to the book of face reading, having a broken tooth contributes to a loss of wealth."

"You want a …?" I began to ask.

"I wonder if I can ask you for a talisman which can help me grow a new tooth to replace the old one."

"Ha!" I laughed, "You need a dentist to help you with that!"

Jiang Wei said, "It is costly to consult a dentist. Without the root of the tooth, you need a fixed-bridge supported by the adjacent left and right teeth. Thus, it is best that I grow a new tooth."

"There is no such thing as growing a new tooth, you know. You are not a kid anymore."

"I heard you are able to solve any problem."

"Nonsense!"

"It's not nonsense. It's true," Jiang Wei said.

I told Jiang Wei, "What I have here are talismans to help an infant's teeth come through, to cure toothaches, and to treat inflammation of the gums as well as tooth decay. Your condition doesn't seem to fit into any of these."

"All I need is a talisman to grow a new tooth."

"No way," I said.

"Why not?"

"They only work for infants and you're not a baby."

Jiang Wei said, "I'd like to give it a try!"

"The effectiveness of talismans depends on the sincerity of one's heart. There is no room for frivolous attempts."

"But my heart is sincere when I request a talisman that can help grow a tooth."

"That's for an infant," I repeated.

"Why don't you treat me as an infant baby then?" Jiang Wei insisted.

"If the talisman doesn't work, don't blame me."

"I won't."

I could not refuse Jiang Wei's repeated request. I drew a talisman for him that helped grow new teeth, which was meant for infants. Naturally, the talisman had no effect on him.

Any infant whose teeth have not come through needs only this talisman to help push the teeth out. It works every time.

Jiang Wei was not about to give up so easily. He came to see me again.

"My friends told me you have the best solutions for everything and that you have great power," Jiang Wei said. "What is impossible miraculously becomes possible in your hands. I hope you can create a miracle for me."

"To make an adult grow a new tooth? Aren't you stretching it a little too far?" I said.

"That would be a miracle. A true miracle."

I finally told Jiang Wei, "Alright! I do know that within Vajrayana teachings, there is a Bodhisattva known as Vajrayaksa [also known as Vajra Teeth Bodhisattva]. I'll consult him and ask him how to help an adult grow a new tooth. Who knows, he may have a solution for you."

Jiang Wei left happily.

To help Jiang Wei, I picked an auspicious time and date to construct a shrine for Vajrayaksa Bodhisattva. In the shrine I placed a lotus throne for Vajrayaksa Bodhisattva, together with the offerings of incense, flowers, perfume, lamps, tea and fruits.

I chanted the Mantra of Purifying the Dharma Realms:

[transliteration:] Om, nam, so-ha
[Sanskrit: OM NAM SVAHA].

I formed the Vajrayaksa Bodhisattva Mudra and visualized the Bodhisattva descending onto the shrine to receive my offerings. [I chanted:]

May this scent of fragrant flowers permeate the dharma realms throughout the Ten Directions
To all buddhas and saints dwelling in the countless pure lands
Please accept this offering and extend your help
Please deliver sentient beings from their suffering
And help them attain enlightenment together

Devas of earth, water, fire, and wind, I summon you to appear
May the requested deities respond immediately to this summons
I sincerely invoke the presence of Vajrayaksa
Transforming this offering to present to you

I saw Vajrayaksa Bodhisattva descending from above, promptly seated on a precious lotus throne. His golden body emanated endless circles of light.

I went straight to the question, "Is there a method to help an adult grow new teeth?"

Vajrayaksa Bodhisattva laughed and said, "Are you aware of the reason I have Vajra Teeth?"

"I only know about the teeth, but I do not know what the teeth are used for."

"I, Vajrayaksa Bodhisattva, am not here to help anyone grow new teeth. My Vajra Teeth symbolize the strength and toughness of teeth that grinds away all demonic hindrances. The teeth also symbolize the crushing of all the greed, anger and ignorance of humans. I will bite all demons and ghosts into pieces if they dare to approach me and thus, the teeth represent crushing all evils."

"I understand now," I said.

Vajrayaksa Bodhisattva continued, "Ekajati, with her single tuft of hair, one eye, and one tooth, also symbolizes this, as do the teeth of Hayagriva. Together, we form the Trinity of Teeth."

"Is there a way to help an adult grow new teeth?" I asked.

"No."

"Who should I approach for help?"

"I don't know."

I saw Vajrayaksa Bodhisattva off and knew the fact that no bodhisattvas of the Ten Directions or any wise beings could offer a way to grow new teeth for an adult. Even the Trinity of Teeth could not offer a method.

I thought I knew everything. I thought I understood the ways of heaven and earth, the ways of human beings, the teachings of the Dharma, and all principles. In the end I realized how little I actually knew. I knew nothing and could do nothing. I was such an ignorant fool!

I thought of how the buddhas and bodhisattvas express their compassion. We need to help remove and transform the suffering of all sentient beings and do it with the greatest joy. Besides purifying our own karma, we need to help others purify their karma.

When we help others resolve their karma, we need to enlighten them on the underlying causes and effects that affect them as they journey through life. We need to untie the knots of karma that bind us.

Only when karma is purified can the knots be unraveled. When all karma is resolved and Buddha-nature surfaces, and when Buddha-nature reveals itself through your cultivation, you are enlightened. Thus, helping ourselves and others find enlightenment is a sign of a truly compassionate bodhisattva.

Having said this, I want to stress that to help save the world, you need to gain the ability, or attainment, for the task. At least I am surrounded with guardian deities, Skanda, dharma protectors, wrathful protectors, Yamantaka, many virtuous gods and heavenly nagas.

When I give an order, they will carry it out. We must have the ability to remove the sufferings of people so that we can lead them through the door of Buddhism. These are realistic issues and if you cannot help solve these matters, people are not going to have faith in you.

What I mean is that many embrace Buddhism because the Dharma answers their wishes.

Take the example of Jiang Wei. He requested a new tooth. If he had no new tooth, he would not listen to you at all. If he had a new tooth, he would embrace Buddhism. That's how things are when you want to lead people to the Buddhist teachings.

Thus:

Few walk the path to the Western Paradise
Just one recitation of Amitabha's name denotes the highest teaching
To lead people to Buddhism, you need spiritual responses
If one receives a response, one is most willing to cultivate

That was why I was so eager to help Jiang Wei, but I realized I was unable to help him; I simply did not know how.

Despite the fact that I know the ways of heaven and earth, I blamed myself for not being able to help him grow a new tooth. There are so many deities and bodhisattvas and yet none of them could help out. How were they supposed to save the world?

Could the Buddhadharma open Jiang Wei's mouth and implant a new tooth into his gums so that it may grow? Or would a buddha simply utter a magic word and out comes a new tooth? If there were no supernatural power, then how would one convince anyone of anything?

I was really depressed. The next time I met with Jiang Wei, I told him, "I doubt you can grow a new tooth."

"What? But they say you can solve everything!"

"It's just impossible," I was blushing.

"So much for supernatural power!" He was blaming me.

"Okay!" I said to him, "I'll teach you a mantra. It's a very good mantra. All you need to do is to chant it one hundred thousand times and your wish will be fulfilled. If you chant it three hundred fifty thousand times, you will attain siddhi and leave behind all illnesses and disasters. If you chant more, all demonic hindrances will be eradicated. If you complete chanting it eight million times, you will be reborn in the Western Pure Land of Ultimate Bliss."

Jiang Wei was moved.

"Okay. I only want my wish fulfilled."

So I taught him the mantra:

OM GURU LIAN SHENG SIDDHI HUM.

"What kind of mantra is this?"

"It's the Heart Mantra of Padmakumara, also known as the Teeth Growing Mantra," I said.

"Padmakumara or no Padmakumara, I am not interested. What counts is that I get a new tooth."

So Jiang Wei began chanting the mantra and he was absolutely devoted. He would bathe and cleanse himself, light incense, sit properly with his palms together, clear his thoughts and visualize a buddha appearing in the sky above him. The buddha would radiate light on Jiang Wei and he would visualize a new tooth growing in his mouth.

He would then chant:

OM GURU LIAN SHENG SIDDHI HUM.

After chanting one hundred thousand times, he dreamed of a bodhisattva descending from heaven. The bodhisattva asked him some interesting questions.

"Why do you hit the drum?"

"If I don't, it wouldn't make a sound," he replied.

"What brings you here?" the bodhisattva asked.

"I am missing a tooth. How am I supposed to open my mouth without it?"

"Since you sounded the drum, I will fill the missing tooth in for you," the bodhisattva answered.

The bodhisattva placed his hand on Jiang Wei's head and gave him a blessing. He then proceeded to touch his face and pressed on the area around his mouth.

Jiang Wei instantly felt a sense of relief and lightness. His gums seemed to harden and a tooth appeared to be growing.

Then, the strangest thing happened. Since that dream, Jiang Wei felt his gums hardening. In between the gap where the old tooth was, a white spot appeared. As the white spot grew larger, it became evident that a new tooth was emerging.

Miracle! A miracle indeed!

This was simply incredible.

Jiang Wei came to inform me of the news and I said nothing. I only mentioned that once a seventy-three-year-old Nyingma lama had lost most of his teeth. The lama recited the Seven Syllable Heart Mantra from the Padma family of Buddhas, **[transliteration:] Om, ah-lu-li-ge, so-ha [Sanskrit: OM ARURUIGA SVAHA]**, countless times and his gums grew seven teeth. This incident was well known in Tibet and was told to me by a Tibetan rinpoche.

I was happy for Jiang Wei. Actually, when Jiang Wei's gums began to harden, I had my own interesting experience. My lower left wisdom tooth began aching.

I visited the dentist and he told me he could not diagnose the cause of my toothache. There was no decay in the wisdom tooth and no inflammation of the gums. The nerve was not infected and the wisdom tooth remained strong and firm.

The dentist gave me an injection to relieve the pain. However, the pain returned when the effects of the anesthetic wore off.

I felt uncomfortable. I knew how to draw a talisman to stop toothaches and hence I drew one with great sincerity. I burned it and drank the talisman ashes with water. Normally, this talisman was very effective, but it did not work on me. Despite several repeated attempts to take the talisman as a pain-killer, the pain remained.

I experienced first-hand the saying, "A toothache is not an illness, but its pain can kill you."

I returned to the dentist and he said, "Anyway, you need to pull your wisdom tooth when you reach a certain age, and it's long overdue for you. I suggest you get rid of it once and for all."

"Okay," I said.

Once the tooth was removed, the pain was gone.

On the very day my tooth was removed, Jiang Wei's new tooth came through.

Someone asked me, "Grand Master Lu, are you taking on Jiang Wei's karma?"

I laughed. Was it substitution of karma or simply a coincidence? I did not have the answer.

I felt that it was kind of a waste to chant a mantra merely to grow a tooth. Padmakumara Heart Mantra can deliver one to the Pure Land and allow one to attain the very siddhi that I have personally attained and verified. I am not lying. If you chant the heart mantra of Padmakumara, you will become Padmakumara himself.

It was good to know that Jiang Wei did not stop his chanting and has since gained greater faith in this mantra. He told people, "This mantra brings great benefits and it's simply amazing."

Here is a verse:

Don't hesitate to chant mantras
Its power can eradicate all karmic hindrances
Behold! The world of samsara is just a prison
Fame and fortune are but candles melting in the flame
Birth, aging, sickness, and death run in a natural cycle
All ties of love and relationships come and go
Thus, engage yourself in cultivation through chanting
When the time comes, you will find paradise within reach

This verse is a wake-up call.

Few walk the path to the Western Paradise
Just one recitation of Amitabha's name denotes the highest teaching
To lead people to Buddhism, you need spiritual responses
If one receives a response, one is most willing to cultivate

Sheng-yen Lu

5 Avoiding a Mudslide

Once, I had a discussion about Buddhism with Venerable Zhaoyin.

"Grand Master Lu, you claim that you're enlightened. May I ask what enlightenment is?"

I replied, "It is beyond words."

"How does one know?"

"You know what you experience, whether it is warm or cold."

"Even a three-year-old can say that!" Venerable Zhaoyin said.

"Yes, indeed. But you need to ask yourself whether or not you are truly free within."

"Does the Tao have a form?"

"As it is, the Tao is formless."

"If the Tao is formless, how does it seek its balance?" Venerable Zhaoyin asked.

"It does it naturally."

Having practiced Zen for the past twenty years, Venerable Zhaoyin thought he could shut me up once and for all by discussing the Buddhadharma with me. All it would take is one small mistake with my words and he would go for the kill.

I smiled, remaining firm in my verbal defense.

"Grand Master Lu, you are neither preaching Buddhism nor Taoism. People criticize you!"

"Let me ask you this: is the highest peak connected with the deepest sea?"

The Venerable Zhaoyin said, "Why do you have to include the spirits?"

"As mighty as the universe may be, it is nothing more than a bubble," I uttered.

Venerable Zhaoyin could not question me any further.

This time, he asked, "Grand Master Lu. You claim you have supernatural power. Can you offer me some proof?"

"I wish to save your life!" I uttered.

"Save my life?" Unconvinced, Venerable Zhaoyin sneered at me and said, "I can liberate myself. I don't need your help."

"Whether you can liberate yourself or not is not an urgent issue. You have a pending disaster coming your way."

"Rubbish! This is just one of those fortune-teller tricks."

"Whether you believe it or not, it's all up to you."

"Alright then, go ahead and tell me about it!"

"There are four men in black who are near you, and they want to take your life!"

"How do I protect myself?"

"Chant the Marici Bodhisattva Mantra."

"I have learned and chanted this mantra before, but I stopped chanting it a long time ago."

I spoke in no uncertain terms to the monk, "Chant the Marici Bodhisattva Mantra:

[transliteration:] Om, mo-li-ji-yi, so-ha
[Sanskrit: OM MARICI YEH SVAHA]."

I added, "When you chant the mantra, you must also recite the following:

> **Protect me against troubles from any ruler.**
> **Protect me from thieves.**
> **Protect me in my travels.**
> **Protect me from disasters of fire and water.**
> **Protect me from harm in wars.**
> **Protect me from psychic attacks.**
> **Protect me from being poisoned.**
> **Protect me from wild beasts, poisonous insects and all enemies.**
> **Protect me in all places and at all times."**

Venerable Zhaoyin said, "You saw four men in black around me and I see nothing. You want me to recite the Marici Bodhisattva Mantra. I can do this. You say that I will encounter a disaster. If nothing happens to me, I will expose you as a fraud, and your so-called enlightenment will be reduced to nothing more than just your own personal understanding."

I told him, "It's really up to you."

The Venerable Zhaoyin clasped his palms and left.

Actually, when the monk first approached me, I had immediately sensed that he would face a disaster. That was because there were four men in black, who were spiritual officials, waiting for him.

These four spiritual officials were ahead of the monk, and they wanted to rush into my house. I stopped them before they could enter and they had to linger around the vicinity as they were waiting for him.

This is how I secretly save many sentient beings. Many face calamities and they do not necessarily know about them. I would not let them know. I help them resolve their situations without their knowledge.

Actually, there is bound to be some degree of calamity in our lives. Shakyamuni Buddha foresaw this when he said, "Human life is one of uncertainty."

Thus:

> **The Three Realms of existence are engulfed in scorching flames**
> **Even the ordained are not guaranteed safety**
> **Impermanence awaits one continuously**
> **Calm your thoughts and prepare yourself for the final journey**

I am aware that people are afraid of calamity and disaster. Thus, I cultivate daily and secretly help many people get through their adversities. I chanted the Marici Bodhisattva Mantra, and I dedicated the merits to Venerable Zhaoyin. With my help, Venerable Zhaoyin would be saved.

* * *

Venerable Zhaoyin lived alone in a small hut, deep within Bagua Mountain in Changhua, Taiwan.

He practiced Zen meditation and sat cross-legged in the lotus position.

The monk was once a student studying abroad in Japan. While in Japan, he developed a strong interest in Buddhism and was ordained as a monk in a famous Soto Zen monastery in Kyoto. His lineage thus came from Japan.

After a dispute over the Dharma robe [which signified transmission of the Dharma], the Sixth Patriarch Huineng did not pass it on. Zen blossomed into the "Five Houses" [in China, where it is known as Chan], which are the Linji sect [Japanese: Rinzai Zen], Caodong sect [Wade Giles: T'sao Tung; Japanese: Soto Zen], Guiyang sect, Yunmen sect, and Fayan sect.

Zen Buddhism is known as the teaching of the heart.

The name Chan [later to be known as Zen in Japan and in the West] was adopted for this school of Buddhism during the beginning of the Tang Dynasty. Zen means cultivation of one's thoughts, which is the process of contemplating truth itself. This is a practice of serenity and concentration.

The First Zen Patriarch in China was Bodhidharma, an Indian man who went to China during the Liang Dynasty to transmit the School of Buddha's Heart and Mind teachings. His method emphasized the importance of serene meditation and inward contemplation, expressing the Buddha Mind and focusing on the practice of concentration and purification. In so doing, the method gives the impression of sitting in meditation; hence it is called Zen Buddhism.

Zen Buddhism stresses the following:

Omission of the written language
Direct revelation of the mind
Attaining buddhahood through seeing Buddha-nature and
Active discussion on Prajna, or wisdom

One stormy night, Venerable Zhaoyin was meditating alone in his hut. The rain had been pouring for three consecutive days and nights. Venerable Zhaoyin was aware that water was accumulating in the marketplace at the foot of the mountain. If the rain persisted, a flood would be inevitable.

Suddenly, the cry of a child was heard outside the hut, and the sound intermingled with the pouring rain.

"Mommy! Mommy!"

Venerable Zhaoyin raised his head and listened.

"Mommy! Mommy!" The words kept repeating and it was definitely a child's cry.

As he listened closely, it became: "Marici! Marici! Marici!"

He recited a line of the mantra,

[transliteration:] Om, mo-li-ji-yi, so-ha
[Sanskrit: OM MARICI YEH SVAHA].

In the mist of the heavy downpour, Venerable Zhaoyin quickly got up and put on his raincoat and rain boots. He grabbed a flashlight and hurried out of his hut to search for the crying child.

"Mommy! Marici!"

Was it mommy or Marici? He was confused.

The cry came from the front, then from the back, and then switched from the left to the right. It was as if someone was playing hide-and-seek with him.

He walked for an hour in the storm.

Suddenly, the cry disappeared. He waited for a long time and listened. There was not a sound [of a child crying] anywhere, and he then realized there was nobody living in this area. If there were no family living in this mountainous area, what would be the chances of finding any child crying around here?

Venerable Zhaoyin rushed back to his hut, only to find that it was gone. A mudslide had buried the hut under a pile of rocks and mud, forming a small hill.

Rocks and mud kept sliding downwards from the mountaintop, and he found himself in extreme danger. Frightened, Venerable Zhaoyin fled the area where he had spent two years meditating.

His life was spared, but his hut, together with all his possessions, were gone.

Upon reflection, Venerable Zhaoyin realized that he had to go through this calamity. He remembered that this was prophesied by Living Buddha Lian-sheng, Sheng-yen Lu. The four spiritual officials in black clothing were waiting to arrest him. It was because of the suggestion of Living Buddha Lian-sheng that he seriously chanted the Marici Bodhisattva Mantra as his protection mantra.

Although Venerable Zhaoyin practices Zen, he was exposed to the teachings of other schools of Buddhism in his life. He chanted the Marici Bodhisattva Mantra in his younger days, and was now able to continue chanting the mantra upon my suggestion.

As the saying goes:

If you burn the incense, you will be protected
If you consume food, you will be energized
Mommy
Marici
They sound alike

* * *

After leaving Bagua Mountain, Venerable Zhaoyin took shelter with various temples and monasteries all over Taiwan. He was used to living the life of a hermit and cultivating alone in his little hut, engaging in ascetic-like practices. After experiencing the calamity, he switched from being a hermit to living among others. This was a new experience for him.

He met many fellow cultivators and heard Living Buddha Liansheng, Sheng-yen Lu mentioned a lot. Generally speaking, most would choose to criticize me, and these negative impressions would spread. Thus, most practitioners tend to reject me and only a handful choose to reserve their comments. This is the state of affairs in religious circles.

Venerable Zhaoyin listened but kept his views to himself. When others called me a mara or a heretic, he sat in silence, knowing the truth about what had happened. He wanted to clear my name but being outnumbered, he would not stand a chance against them. He decided to save his breath and remained silent throughout the conversation.

Venerable Zhaoyin visited me and mentioned what he had heard.

He said, "Why don't you change your approach to liberate sentient beings and use a new and different way altogether? You can start building a new foundation."

I replied, "People have already made up their minds about me. It may seem easy to start all over again, but it would take a lot of effort and time to change things."

"You must at least have some hope!"

"Once people make up their minds about you, it's going to stay that way. I'm used to this and it doesn't matter."

"You don't think it's necessary?" Venerable Zhaoyin asked.

"No, I don't. I take slander and criticism as my own spiritual discipline!"

"But your reputation suffers!"

"Reputation is immaterial in the light of one's spiritual discipline, which is needed for the attainment of buddhahood."

Venerable Zhaoyin nodded.

I told Venerable Zhaoyin, "When I was about to descend from the mountain and leave my master, Reverend Liaoming, he told me that a person like me has only three options in life. The first option is to enter nirvana immediately. The second option is to live in seclusion deep in the mountains, never to appear again. The last option is to act as a fool among people."

"Oh!"

I smiled and continued, "I am happy and content with myself and I don't care what others say about me."

"Do you have regrets?" Venerable Zhaoyin asked.

"No!"

"Do the slanders hurt?"

"No!"

"What about praise and ridicule, misery and honor?"

"They mean nothing to me! Life is but a game to me, and I merely experience it to the fullest."

Venerable Zhaoyin invited me to ascend to my teaching seat with the greatest respect, and then he sincerely prostrated before me three times.

"Why do you prostrate?"

"To thank you for saving my life!"

"I didn't save you. You saved yourself!"

"But I still needed your guidance on what to do!"

I remained silent.

Venerable Zhaoyin told me this before leaving my place: "I feel like leaving this human world of suffering."

I told him, "It's all in your heart. If your heart is free, then that is truly leaving this world behind."

"You mean I should adjust and adapt to this world?"

"No! There is no world to begin with," I said.

Venerable Zhaoyin contemplated this for a while, and finally nodded his head. He realized what I meant and said, "I understand this in principle, but putting it into practice and eventually mastering this art constitutes a True Buddha!"

Here's a verse:

One, two, three, four, five, six, seven
Still the mind and ascend to the Western Pure Land
It seems so easy when the words of Buddha are spoken
Yet one stumbles, plunging into mud too often

If you burn the incense, you will be protected
If you consume food, you will be energized
Mommy
Marici
They sound alike

Sheng-yen Lu

6 Revoking Dharma Power

Once, I had a rather strange dream. I found myself flying through mountains and ridges. While ascending to the highest peak, I saw a Tibetan rinpoche sitting on a flat platform with two lamas beside him. One of them was hoisting a banner while the other was blowing a trumpet.

I simply floated into the space above and soared freely above the Tibetan rinpoche.

This rinpoche asked the lamas beside him, "Who is that Chinese man?" One lama replied, "He is Living Buddha Lian-sheng, Sheng-yen Lu." The other lama added, "Sheng-yen Lu is very famous and possesses great dharma power. He has been to the Drepung Loseling Monastery in India to give a discourse on the Buddhadharma."

The Tibetan rinpoche paused for a while and then said, "I want to revoke his dharma power."

After having this dream, I had another dream involving the same Tibetan rinpoche.

The rinpoche and I were standing on the bank of a mighty river. The river was turbulent with rolling waters and I could not tell how deep it was.

The buoyancy of this river was considerably poor. I saw a leaf fell into the river and it could not stay afloat. It disappeared into the whirling water in no time. This mighty river was such a dangerous river to cross that even a goose feather would be unable to float on it.

The Tibetan rinpoche said to me, "Sheng-yen Lu, you will demonstrate your dharma power and cross this river first. You are not to fly across, but actually walk on the water."

This was a test of my skill and power.

First, I visualized my lineage gurus above my head. Then, I formed the Heavenly Water Mudra with my hands and recited the Water Resistance Verse:

This water without mercy
Has not carried a person in millennia
Now I will walk across
The massive sea is transformed into a mulberry field
Execute this order at once
Execute this order at once
Execute this order at once

I stepped onto the water and, just as I thought, the water felt like solid ground. Very soon, I reached the other side of the river with no problems along the way at all.

Now it was the Tibetan rinpoche's turn. He hesitated for a moment before taking a bold step and then finally attempted to walk on the water. Then came a sound, "Splash!" He fell right into the water. He was a completely drenched mess.

Just as the Tibetan rinpoche was about to sink to the bottom and drown, the rinpoche's dharma protector, a gigantic Golden-Winged Garuda, came to his rescue. It caught hold of him by his collar, lifted him and placed him on land.

The Tibetan rinpoche was very embarrassed. He turned towards me and said, "I will revoke your dharma power."

These two dreams were very unusual. During that period of time, many Tibetan rinpoches took refuge in me. I conducted a dharma ceremony together with His Holiness the Hundredth Ganden Tripa, the head of the Gelugpa tradition of Tibetan Buddhism. I had a meeting with the Dalai Lama. I ascended the dharma throne and expounded the Buddhadharma at the three largest Tibetan monasteries. I was the only ethnic Chinese to be given this honor.

My reputation spreads far and wide throughout India and Tibet. Many Tibetan rinpoches have taken refuge in me. One of them is Jigme Lhundrup Rinpoche, who was formerly the Chairman of the Sixth Assembly of Tibetan People's Deputies of the Tibetan Government in Exile.

My photo is enshrined in the Ganden Shartse Sockpa Khangtsen Monastery, Drepung Tsawa Khangtsen Monastery and others.

I figure this will certainly establish a deep affinity with Tibetan Buddhism. This is naturally a good thing because my lineage transmission comes from Tibet through Nora Rinpoche [also known as Gara Lama], Reverend Liaoming, Thubten Nyima, Thubten Tare, Thubten Dargye, the Sixteenth Karmapa, His Eminence Sakya Zhengkong Lama and others.

But likewise, there are some drawbacks to this. Because my dharma power and my reputation are too widespread, this results in attracting much resentment.

Of course, even rinpoches can be disgruntled by it. I felt that the rinpoche in my two dreams was discontented as he had repeatedly said that he wanted to revoke my dharma power. These two dreams came as a wake-up call and appeared inauspicious.

Thus:

Without realizing the original unchanging nature
Playing the role of a dharma king is but a worthless pursuit

Unenlightened, yet in this place one dwells
How could anyone ever realize True Suchness
By scrambling to be the best and most powerful

* * *

I have been cultivating Vajrayana Buddhism, setting up shrines, reciting mantras, achieving spiritual response by body, speech and mind, eradicating negative karma, increasing wisdom and transforming from the mundane into the holy. Such merits and spiritual powers are inconceivable.

I have received the very heart essence that flows from the heart of Vairocana as he transcends the past, the present and the future, and imparts the inner secret doctrine to Vajrasattva, among others, at the Most Victorious Dharmadhatu Palace of the Akanistha Heaven.

After receiving the empowerments from many masters and acquiring the secrets of the dharma, I expounded the Vajrayana teachings, founded True Buddha School and established the seats or places of cultivation (the mandala). Only the buddhas know of my achievement.

I know the great merits I have cultivated are literally unheard of in this world. As such, I am true nature itself.

Thus:

The four levels of secret I expound
Are very intricate and deeply profound
The three karmas of body, speech and mind
Are transformed through the ways of Vajrayana
How mysterious and esoteric they are

These two dreams were clear and vividly real. As my consciousness is one and the same as the Buddha-nature itself - complete, undifferentiated in nature and creating no illusions or karma-such dreams are naturally different from those of an ordinary person.

Besides dreaming, my meditation revealed an interesting vision. I found myself walking in the nether world. There was no lamp to help navigate my path. An inner light radiating from within my heart lit the way.

In addition, three golden lamps floated above my head. These are the lights of my lineage transmissions.

Suddenly, a giant garuda came soaring in the sky above. It dived and snatched away the three golden lamps with its beak. Fierce beasts were roaring around me and sounded extremely horrifying. Blood-curdling screams and cries were heard from many evil ghosts. What a frightening world it was.

I saw a mighty dharma protector, riding on a horse and wearing a straw hat. He was none other than Dorje Shugden. I was surprised. These visions came as a flash and disappeared, leaving me puzzled and confused.

Soon after, a certain Sonam Lama visited me from India and secretly told me, "There is trouble, Living Buddha Lian-sheng."

"What trouble?"

"A khenpo, an abbot by the name of Chod Khang Rinpoche, who possesses great dharma power and holds a senior position, is going to perform a rite to revoke your dharma power."

"Chod Khang Rinpoche?" I thought for a moment and said, "I don't know this person."

"You don't know him, but he knows you," Sonam Lama said.

"Why does he want to revoke my dharma power?" I was perplexed.

"Because you are too famous."

"It's not my wish to be famous."

"Chod Khang Rinpoche feels that you have stepped onto his turf."

"I hold no territory myself."

"When you went to India, you did not pay him a visit!"

"At which monastery was he residing?"

"You visited Drepung Monastery and then Ganden Monastery, but you did not visit Sera Monastery. Chod Khang Rinpoche is outraged. He will surely teach you a good lesson!"

"Is not visiting him a crime?"

"Yes."

"How powerful is this Chod Khang Rinpoche?" I asked.

Sonam Lama said, "Chod Khang Rinpoche became famous at an early age as a sorcerer in Tibet. He established his fame early on and defeated many sorcerers. Once he casts his spell, his opponent will either die immediately from vomiting blood, or suffer from a tormenting illness. Others have fallen while riding horses and suffered great injuries. Still others have fallen off cliffs and died, and so on."

"That's quite powerful!" I exclaimed.

Sonam Lama said, "To my knowledge, Chod Khang Rinpoche has two major dharma protectors. One of them is the most famous Dorje Shugden and the other is the Great Golden-Winged Garuda. These two great dharma protectors render him unrivaled."

"Dorje Shugden," I remarked, "Isn't there an order banning this cultivation?"

Sonam Lama replied, "Tibetan Buddhism has split into two factions over this controversy. One faction bans this cultivation while the other allows it. However, the practice of Dorje Shugden enables one to have great dharma power in a relatively short time. Thus, more and more people are drawn to cultivating the Dorje Shugden practice. This crisis is threatening to split up the community of Tibetan Buddhism."

I was greatly shaken by these words from Sonam Lama, but I felt no fear because I believed that "a clear conscience has no fear of evil."

Sonam Lama said, "You must take precautions!"

"But how?"

"By summoning one dharma protector to fight against another dharma protector!" Sonam Lama said.

After giving me this warning, Sonam Lama left in a hurry. I took this warning from Sonam Lama very seriously because it somehow tied in with the two recent dreams I had. However, when faced with such a pressing issue, you can only stay alert, and remain still and unmoved in the eye of the storm.

* * *

As expected, Dorje Shugden came, and this was how he appeared:

While the four hooves of his horse step magnificently
Unperturbed, he supports the sky with his straw hat
He roams freely without barriers
Riding his horse impressively up into the highest clouds

Dorje Shugden took direct aim at the top of my head with a vajra. If I were just an ordinary cultivator, a blow from Dorje Shugden would have fatally crushed my head, sending me to report to Lord Yama.

However, I regularly engage in my dharma protector practice, thus Yamantaka is always by my side. Naturally, Yamantaka will appear above my head and shield me in all directions. Yamantaka appears in a wrathful form with many heads, arms and legs.

I observed the situation and realized if I had to summon Yamantaka to fight Dorje Shugden, there would be nothing wrong with it. But why let it come to that point?

I instructed Yamantaka to step back immediately.

I willed my skull to break open into eight petals. A cracking sound was heard and my skull unfolded like a lotus in full bloom. Sitting in meditation on the lotus was Amitabha Buddha himself, manifesting all of his thirty-two major and eighty minor physical marks.

Thus:

Just as the lotus pond that reflects the moon mirrors only emp-

tiness
And the bamboo forest seems to sing as the wind blows across it
How many cultivators living on Earth
Have mistakenly thought Amitabha resides on another mountain peak

When Dorje Shugden realized it was none other than the Amitabha Tathagata himself in all his compassion and radiance, blossoming like a single lotus in the lotus kingdom, he quickly withdrew his vajra, held his palms together in respect and left.

Thus, a battle was averted.

At first, I assumed that when Dorje Shugden left, this matter had concluded, but that was not the case.

Whenever I cultivate, first comes my invocation:

[transliteration:] Om, si-ba-wa, su-da, sa-er-wa, da-er-ma, si-ba-wa, su-do, hang
[Sanskrit: OM SOBHAWA SHUDDHA SARVA DHARMA SOBHAWA SHUDDHO HAM].

And then add:

[transliteration:] Om, ah, hum, so-ha
[Sanskrit: OM AH HUM SVAHA].

The deities that I invoke will usually manifest themselves. But this time, they were nowhere to be found. There was no sign of them whatsoever. I thought it was very strange. It seemed that my mantra power had disappeared.

So, I summoned the presence of the most fundamental deities - the Earth Deities of the Four Directions:

> **[transliteration:] Namo san-man-do, moo-toh-nam, om, doo-loo doo-loo, dei-wei, so-ha**
> **[Sanskrit: NAMO SAMANTA BUDDHANAM OM DURU DURU DEVI SVAHA].**

I formed a mudra with my hands and stomped my foot on the ground. Usually, the Earth Deities of the Four Directions would immediately appear. Yet, this time they did not show up. It seemed that my chanting had fallen on deaf ears and was not working at all. It was as good as not reciting the mantra at all. I was really worried. My dharma power had disappeared. Feeling like a punctured ball, I could not effectively exercise my power.

Usually, I made my offering and recited the Elixir (or Nectar) Mantra:

> **[transliteration:] Namo su-lu-ba-ya, da-ta-ga, da-ya, da-di-ya-ta, om, su-lu, su-lu, bo-la, su-lu, bo-la, su-lu, so-ha**
> **[Sanskrit: NAMO SURUPAYA TATHAGATAYA TADYATHA OM SURU SURU PRASURU PRASURU SVAHA].**

As I sprinkled the nectar, spiritual beings would gather to receive the offering. Yet none came. The water was simply water and not the elixir it should have been.

Now this was serious! The Food Transformation Mantra that I had recited was also ineffective. My attempts to summon any deities were futile. Chanting and empowering the Great Compassion Dharani Water did not work. No matter which mantra I chanted, none of them worked. I had indeed lost all of my mantra power. Losing all of one's power of mantra was scary. It meant that I was no better than an ordinary mortal being.

I thought about my ability of seeking divination through my fingers, as I wanted to find the cause of this predicament. I extended my hand and prayed to the deities who were passing by to give me some directions. How strange! My fingers did not dance and quiver. Without the spiritual current, I cannot get a divination, as this type of divination requires that the fingers bend automatically. If they don't, then I cannot make divinations!

I looked up at the sky above. The sky, being the sky, was empty. Suddenly, it occurred to me that the three golden lamps above my head were nowhere to be seen. These three golden lamps were the symbolic manifestation of my lineage transmission empowerment. How could they have disappeared?

It then occurred to me that while I was busy facing Dorje Shugden, the Great Golden-Winged Garuda secretly stole the lamps. This situation tied in with my dreams. I realized that once the power of lineage transmission was gone, no mantra could ever work.

The book *Doctrinal Essentials of Vajrayana* states:

> **"The Vajrayana school arises from divine wisdom realized by the Buddha and transmitted directly to the mortals of this Saha (or human) world. Vajrayana cultivators receive a surge in spiritual strength and gain inconceivable power. However, Vajrayana emphasizes heavily on the lineage transmission power and anyone who wishes to cultivate it must enter into the Great Mandala and receive the empowerment from a vajra master. Only then will he have the power of the lineage transmission. Without this power of lineage transmission, all mantras will be void, rendering all practices as theft of the dharma."**

It also says:

> **"The lineage transmission power is the very root of Vajrayana practice. It comes from the cosmic universe and awakens the very wisdom that lies within the heart. This is the root wisdom of the**

Vajrayana lineage transmission."

In order to regain my dharma power, I realized I had to get back my three golden lamps. This meant I had to face Chod Khang Rinpoche. I felt that this Chod Khang Rinpoche was really powerful and I really did not want to reveal my personal deity [Tibetan: yidam] to demand the return of my three golden lamps. This would go against my personality.

What could I do then?

Fortunately, I am a Vajrayana lineage holder and I am well aware of secrets beyond all secrets. Even though the three golden lamps had been stolen, I would still be able to light up three more golden lamps. I could manifest immeasurable numbers of these three golden lamps.

The Dharani Sutra of the Great Wheel (Mahachakra) Vajra says:

> **"Recite this mantra twenty one times and you will achieve success in all mantra cultivation. All virtuous deeds will swiftly be accomplished. This mantra also helps complete the attainment of all mudra practices. In all mandala practices, one enters the great mandala shrine without the need of an actual shrine."**

The Sutra of Collection of Dharani states:

> **"Recite this mantra twenty one times, and one will gain entrance into any mandala and attain all accomplishments. Body mudra[yoga postures, asanas], among other mudra exercises, may accompany mantra recitation. If a hand mudra is formed while reciting a mantra, it will be easier to obtain results. If one has not entered the shrine of empowerment, one cannot form any hand mudra. However, when one recites this mantra, it is equivalent to entering the Tantric shrine. Forming a mudra for practice would not be stealing from the dharma."**

The Great Tibetan Essential Tantra states:

> **"According to the dharma, all mantras and mudras must be transmitted by the guru. Prior to entering the empowerment shrine, forming any mudra for any practice constitutes an act of dharma theft. All of one's practices will yield no results. However, if one recites this mantra twenty one times before the statue of the Tathagata, it would be as good as seeing the Buddha himself and entering into all mandalas. All dharma requested for practice will gain success and attainment."**

I immediately reviewed the Great Wheel Vajra Mantra [Mahachakra Dharani] and visualized all my lineage transmission masters above me transforming into the three golden lamps.

I recited the Great Wheel Vajra Mantra:

> **[transliteration:] Namo, si-de-li-ya, ti-wei-ga-lan, da-ta-ga-ta-lan, om, wei-la-ji-wei-la-ji, ma-ha-jia-ge-la, fa-ji-li, sa-da-sa-da, sa-la-de-sa-la-de, de-la-yi-de-la-yi, wei-da-ma-ni, san-ban-gu-ni, de-la-ma-di, xi-da, ge-li-ya, de-lan, so-ha**
> **[Sanskrit: NAMO SITRIYA TIVIKANAM TATHAGATANAM OM VIRAJI VIRAJI MAHACHAKRA VAJRI SADA SADA SARATI SARATI DARIYI DARIYI VIDAMANI SAMBAJANI TRAMATI SIDDHA GRIYA DERAM SVAHA].**

I recited this mantra twenty one times. I looked up and saw not only three, but innumerable glittering golden lamps, forming a vajra chain.

The current was reconnected, and I unleashed the highest force of dharma power.

The golden lamps above emit a thousand rays
From the light, countless lotuses bloom and hover
All dharma power is fulfilled and complete
Sparkling like pearls, shining as exquisitely as jade

It was said that Chod Khang Rinpoche found that the three golden lamps he stole from me through the Great Golden-Winged Garuda suddenly flew into the sky and vanished.

Chod Khang Rinpoche invoked Dorje Shugden, but Dorje Shugden ignored him and refused to be summoned.

Chod Khang Rinpoche's face turned black; his vital energy weakened. As a result, he fell sick three times and has had to struggle with a lingering illness ever since. He became a wretched old man.

Chod Khang Rinpoche told people, "You can challenge any sorcerer except Living Buddha Lian-sheng, Sheng-yen Lu. His dharma power is simply inconceivable. After losing his three golden lamps, he was able to manifest thousands of golden lamps."

What I really want to say is that I did not cast any spell on Chod Khang Rinpoche. I actually did nothing at all.

The golden lamps above emit a thousand rays
From the light, countless lotuses bloom and hover
All dharma power is fulfilled and complete
Sparkling like pearls, shining as exquisitely as jade

Sheng-yen Lu

7 Springtime in the Swimming Pool

Ever since I was young, I have loved swimming. During the years of my youth I swam in small streams, big rivers, irrigation canals, swimming pools and oceans.

I began swimming using the dog paddle style before moving onto the freestyle, breaststroke, backstroke, sidestroke and, finally, the butterfly stroke and synchronized swimming.

When I was in Taiwan and going on day trips for feng shui consultations, I would jump into any stream I spotted in the mountain and yell in joy upon finding a lake, as the weather was unbearably hot.

When I was in Mexico, I learned how to do deep sea diving. This involved wearing an oxygen tank on my back, strapping a belt of lead around my hips, wearing a full-sized mask and snorkel, and putting fins on my feet. I even learned underwater communication with hand signals.

I have a natural love of water.

One day, I went to a health center for a swim in the swimming pool. It was evening and not a holiday. There was no one in the pool. I took a shower, then changed into my swimwear and swim cap.

As I dipped into the water, I felt very cold and then I shuddered. I did not think much of it because the water was especially cold. I did the breaststroke with my head above water, so I did not need to hold my breath underwater. It was a light and relaxing swim.

Suddenly, I sensed that the water in the pool was rippling strangely. It was as though a wind had blown across the water and ripples began to roll.

A fog appeared in front of me and things seemed unreal.

It seemed like a person was swimming towards me. Yet, this individual ignored my presence, swam straight at me, and then right through me, at which point I felt like I was getting an electrical shock.

I turned around to look, but there was no one to be found. I was the only person in the swimming pool, and I felt a chill up my spine. I noted this reaction and concluded that I had encountered a ghost, and this ghost had actually passed through my body!

Most people will not feel a thing when they encounter a ghost. Upon returning home, they would usually experience a bout of cold and hot fever. They would need to contact someone who can perform a rite to calm the patient's spirit and dispel the negative vibrations. This is typical of a psychic interference.

A psychic interference can lead to nightmares and, in some serious cases, can cause depression, insomnia, and eventually mental problems.

I am no ordinary person. I can expel any negative vibrations and ghost energy lingering in my body with my inner fire, and then everything will be fine. There is no cause for concern.

I had no intention of intervening in this ghostly affair but I realized that many people visit this swimming pool. If anyone encounters a psychic interference, the person is bound to become very sick. Out of compassion, I could not possibly walk away from this and not do something about it.

I climbed up the side of the swimming pool and opened my divine eye to observe. Immediately, I saw a girl in a swimsuit. She looked graceful and enchanting, captivating with a body streamlined in beautiful curves and features. She was truly beautiful, with a fair complexion, enrapturing facial features, and a pair of big eyes.

She was swimming not too far from me. I called out to greet her, "Hi!"

"You can see me? I thought no one can see me!" She was surprised.

"I am Sheng-yen Lu. Of course I can see you."

"I have heard of you."

"What's your name?"

"Everybody calls me Xiaocui."

"Why are you here?"

"I died a sudden death."

"Why don't you leave?"

"I am attached here and cannot leave. If I try to leave this place, there are the Sun Deva (Aditya), Moon Deva (Candra), day patrol deities, night patrol deities, and other deities. A small ghost like me can't roam freely!" Xiaocui said.

"How did you die?"

"When the swimming pool was just completed, I went for a swim. My legs became cramped. Three or four minutes later, I drowned."

"Didn't your family deliver your spirit?"

"My parents had passed away. Only some offerings were made for me at the pool side," Xiaocui said.

I said, "I could do a deliverance ceremony for you and lead you out of your suffering. I have great dharma power."

When Xiaocui heard this, she was overjoyed and kept saying, "Thank you! Thank you!"

* * *

As cultivators, we develop bodhicitta or compassion and this can be expressed through our homage to the Three Jewels and our deliverance of all sentient beings. So back home at my shrine, I set up another small shrine for Ksitigarbha Bodhisattva. Incense, flowers, lamps, tea and fruits were arranged accordingly, and offered wholeheartedly.

In front of the statue of Ksitigarbha Bodhisattva, I set up a plaque for Xiaocui.

I entered into the shrine and sat in meditation:

> **[transliteration:] Om, lan, so-ha**
> **[Sanskrit: OM RAM SVAHA].**
>
> **Om.**

I recited:

> **May this cloud of incense and flowers**
> **Fully pervade the realms of the Ten Directions**
> **May this offering be made to all the buddhas**
> **As well as deities, the dharma, and all sages**
>
> **Throughout boundless pure lands**
> **May you receive this offering and perform the buddha's work**
> **Permeating fragrance to bless all sentient beings**
> **Attaining the perfect enlightenment together**

Countless offerings appeared automatically in the sky. I recited the *Ksitigarbha Sutra* for three days. When I performed this rite, Ksitigarbha Bodhisattva would definitely descend onto the shrine. He would be holding his staff and gradually arrive while standing on a lotus flower. Xiaocui's spirit would be led to the shrine to receive the light emitted from Ksitigarbha Bodhisattva and then would be delivered.

Much to my surprise, despite performing the procedure properly and carefully without missing any steps, Xiaocui's spirit did not arrive.

Ksitigarbha Bodhisattva himself did not show up. I had not offended Ksitigarbha Bodhisattva, so it was hard to imagine that he would not show up at all.

They had no reason to be absent. My shrine may be small and my offerings may be humble, but the dharma power was nonetheless at full force and its invoking power could reach the dharma realms of the Ten Directions. My dharma ceremonies are almost always effective - failures are rare.

Unable to invoke the presence of Xiaocui's spirit and Ksitigarbha Bodhisattva, could it be that my dharma power and mantra chanting have lost their effectiveness? The fact remained that my dharma power was fine. I had to get to the bottom of this situation.

I went to find my sworn brother, Cheng Huang [also known as Patron God of the City]. He specializes in managing lost spirits and wandering ghosts.

I asked him why the dharma ceremony did not work.

Cheng Huang told me, "Don't interfere in Xiaocui's affair!"

"What? Don't interfere?"

"Yes! Just mind your own business."

"I love to get involved when there is injustice!"

Cheng Huang chuckled and said, "You're doing this because she's beautiful, right?"

"Nonsense! I am not a skirt-chaser!" I disputed.

"If you had instead encountered a filthy homeless ghost, would you have still conducted the bardo deliverance?"

I was dumbfounded. Remaining persistent, I said, "The spirit of a pretty lady and that of a filthy, wandering spirit are of equal standing and have no difference when seen from the awakened mind."

Cheng Huang told me, "Don't be fooled by outer appearances!"

Cheng Huang then revealed, "The usual kind of dharma ceremony would not be able to invoke the wondering spirit of Xiaocui. What appears to be the case of a beautiful girl swimming and later drowning because of a leg cramp is in fact a fatal strike by the Five Thunders. These Five Thunders are not limited to just lightning and thunder. Burial in a landslide, drowning, being burned to death, dying in a car accident, and being struck by the elements of metal, wood, water, fire and earth all constitute death by the Five Thunders."

"Why was she struck by the Five Thunders?"

"Xiaocui has her karma. She killed people in her past life!"

"We can certainly deliver the spirit of the person killed!"

"It is not just one person!"

"How many then?"

"Over a hundred people!"

"What! That many!" I was stunned.

Cheng Huang said, "She was very angry over a trivial matter, and so at a banquet she poisoned the soup. More than a hundred people died from the poisoning! Because of this karma, she must suffer death from drowning in water over a hundred times. In addition to that, she must re-experience the agony of drowning on the first and fifteenth of every lunar month as a ghost."

Cheng Huang continued, "Her heart is as venomous as a snake or a scorpion. As a result, she must be prepared to taste her own medicine and suffer." I could not help but sigh over Xiaocui.

* * *

I returned to the swimming pool to swim. I pretended nothing had happened. While swimming, strange things started to happen. The water in the swimming pool would become as chilling cold as ice and this sent a chill up in my spine.

The water in the swimming pool would suddenly turn turbulent like the waves in the ocean. Yet, outside the pool, the wind was not strong. I was the only person swimming and there was no reason why the ripples should be so large. I swallowed a mouthful of water and choked badly.

My swimming stroke has always been excellent. I can kick well with the breaststroke. When I was swimming forward, I suddenly felt that someone was pulling on my leg. My leg was held so that I could not kick. Moreover, I was being pulled downward. When I turned my head to look, my leg was freed. When I turned to face forward, my leg was pulled again. This happened repeatedly and it was very tiring to swim under these conditions.

I dived into the water. Moving forward, it seemed like I was stopped by an invisible net and was unable to go forward. I turned around and bumped into another invisible net, finding no way to retreat. Turning towards the left, I found no outlet. Turning towards the right, I was unable to break out. I realized this was like a fisherman casting his net and I was trapped within. Despite my attempts to maneuver left and right, I could not free myself. I was quickly running out of air.

While I was in the water, I silently chanted the mantra syllable, "Hum."

A ray of blue light pulsated. The net was breached and I dashed out of the water and took a deep breath.

I did not want to play games anymore. I walked towards the shower cubicle in the changing room. When I opened the door of the shower cubicle, I was greatly startled.

Xiaocui was standing in the cubicle; her face appeared pale.

I said, "I want to take a shower."

"I can scrub your back," Xiaocui said tenderly.

"I always shower by myself."

"Will you make an exception?"

"Didn't you have enough fun earlier?" I was getting a little angry.

"I was only playing around. Don't take it seriously," Xiaocui said.

"You don't play around by 'Solidifying All Sides' around someone. This can get people killed. It was a good thing that it was me, because if it had been somebody else, he would have suffocated."

"I was testing your dharma power!"

I looked at Xiaocui. Her soft face, with such tender and fair complexion, coupled with a beautiful body, would attract any man that saw her. How could such a woman be so vicious and venomous?

I asked Xiaocui, "Do you want deliverance?"

"Of course."

"Then why did you kill over one hundred people?"

"It was a moment of foolishness."

"Have you repented?"

"I regret my impulsive act!"

"Since over a hundred people were killed, I'm afraid I can't deliver your spirit."

"Didn't you promise that you would deliver my spirit? You have great dharma power!"

I thought about this. I was quick to promise Xiaocui that I would deliver her from her suffering, telling her that I had great dharma power without first finding out about the causes of the matter. Cheng Huang was right. If the ghost were not Xiaocui but a homeless filthy spirit, would I have done the same thing?

Actually, there are many attractive and enchanting female ghosts who in their previous lives were anything but kind.

They told lies, and weaved all kinds of elaborate lies. They were jealous, envious, narrow-minded, scheming, cruel, unscrupulous and malicious.

When some of these women start scheming, they are more aggressive than men.

When you think of these women, you know they can be adorable. Yet they can be the most terrible and horrifying people. Just take a look at history: how many great men and heroes were destroyed at the hands of women?

I wondered if I should save Xiaocui. I was confused.

In the end, perhaps it was fate that did it. I decided to save her. I had promised to help her right from the beginning and I could not go back on my word.

I went ahead and erected a shrine. The dharma process proceeded as usual. However, I visualized this shrine in my mind multiplying into tens, hundreds and then thousands of shrines. I recited the Thousand Turn Mantra (seven times):

> **[transliteration:] Om, fa-ji-la, gu-he-ya, ga-ba, san-ma-ye, hum [Sanskrit: OM VAJRA GUHERYA GAPA SAMAYA HUM].**

This bardo deliverance would have originally delivered only one person. Yet in an instant, this had become a bardo deliverance for a thousand people. Xiaocui's negative karma only involved over a hundred people.

Then came a flash and the roar of a single thunderclap! I pointed a mudra towards the sky! Over a hundred spirits ascended to heaven.

This ascent to heaven illustrates:

> **Liberating all equally with one mantra, one heart**
> **Making no distinction whether someone is noble or lowly, worthy or foolish**
> **If one's bad karma should be uprooted completely**
> **Apply the great dharma and all will be well**

I saw Ksitigarbha Bodhisattva leading Xiaocui to my shrine. Xiaocui's spirit was entangled with stripes of dark rope-like energy.

I shouted, "The one hundred plus victims that you killed have been delivered and ascended to heaven. Why aren't you ascending towards the heavens?"

Xiaocui said, "Those being liberated are indeed the one hundred plus victims. Yet I remain tied up."

Upon hearing this, I said no more. From the top of my head arose a red Sanskrit syllable "Lan" [Sanskrit: RAM] which turned into a fiery red triangular chakra. This triangular chakra sprouted a gigantic flame towards Xiaocui, scorching her into a heap of ashes.

(Even if Xiaocui had committed the Five Deadly Sins, using this syllable to burn her would have eliminated her of all such karma.)

Burning Xiaocui into ashes destroyed all of her negative karma. I saw a ray of bright light which was as crystal clear as a mani jewel, through which rays of pure light flowed and illuminated all Dharma Realms. Ksitigarbha Bodhisattva was holding this mani jewel as he ascended towards the sky.

Ksitigarbha Bodhisattva said, "Lian-sheng, you're really something. Your use of mantra is excellent!"

I closed my palms in respect and said, "Thank you for your presence Ksitigarbha Bodhisattva."

* * *

In this chapter, I have taught everybody a Vajrayana practice. This major technique is among the most secret.

The cultivator sits upright in a meditation posture and calms his mind, allowing the body and mind to be free from all thoughts of the past, present and future.

This is the Dharma Realm Samadhi.

Visualize the Sanskrit syllable "Lan" [Sanskrit: RAM] on top of your head. It illuminates bright light, shining like a full moon. Then, visualize it being transformed into a triangle, which sprouts fire around it. This triangular flame engulfs your body and mind.

Recite the mantra "Lan" [Sanskrit: RAM] twenty one times. This practice can burn away all negative karma of the cultivator!

In addition to that:

The cultivator first holds the mala or prayer beads on the right hand. Roll it around the left hand and then transfer the mala back to the right hand. Form the Lotus Mudra with the prayer beads inside and move the mudra to the front of the head.

Recite:

> **[transliteration:] Om, lan, so-ha**
> **[Sanskrit: OM RAM SVAHA]** (All is purified).
>
> **[transliteration:] Om, hua-lu-jia-na, ma-la, so-ha**
> **[Sanskrit: OM VAIROCANA MALA SVAHA]** (The mala is cleansed).
>
> **[transliteration:] Om, fa-ji-la, gu-he-ya, ga-ba, san-ma-ye, hum**
> **[Sanskrit: OM VAJRA GUHERYA GAPA SAMAYA HUM]**
> (The Thousand Turn Mantra).

A single recitation is equivalent to a thousand recitations. This is a secret practice, and it is also called the Thousand Wheel Turning Technique, and the Thousand Shrine Turning Method.

According to Cheng Huang, as a karmic consequence of saving and delivering Xiaocui, I will have to return to the human world one more time.

Cheng Huang teased me for being nosy. To intervene too often results in many rebirths. But I am not bothered by this, as my main concern remains saving people.

I have made a great vow to deliver and liberate sentient beings life after life. There is nothing of concern except this. I teach people to recite the Buddha's name, chant mantras, and practice the dharma so that they may be liberated from their suffering. Sentient beings are drowning in the sea of sorrow and are unaware of it. I will work until my last breath to help all beings!

Liberating all equally with one mantra, one heart
Making no distinction whether someone is noble or lowly, worthy or foolish
If one's bad karma should be uprooted completely
Apply the great dharma and all will be well

Sheng-yen Lu

8 The Dog Spirit

A friend of mine once invited me to dinner. The host, Mr. Cao Zong, introduced me to everyone and said, "This is Living Buddha Lian-sheng, Sheng-yen Lu. It is not easy to meet him in person as he is very famous and very busy. He is known for his spiritual abilities and he can solve every difficult situation and problem. Living Buddha Lian-sheng has the divine eye!"

Everyone looked at me and remained silent. During dinner, the host Cao Zong asked, "Living Buddha, can you do a reading and tell us if we're doing fine?"

I scanned the group. Everyone remained quiet, waiting to hear what I had to say. I smiled and said, "Most of you are okay." The host seized on my words and said, "You say most of us are okay, which means some of us are not. Who are you referring to?"

I said, "Can I reveal who it is? No objections?"

"Of course we don't object," everyone agreed.

I said, "This Mr. Pan, Pan Qing, has a little..."

"A little what?"

"He has a strange aura around him."

"Can you be more specific about this aura? Is it one of a sissy, kind of feminine, or one that which simply attracts women..." Everyone was teasing Pan Qing.

Pan Qing then said to me, "What aura? Please be more specific. I really don't mind!"

I told him, "It's the spirit of a dog on your body."

Everyone was stunned. Pan Qing said, "I don't feel anything!"

The host Cao Zong said to me, "Living Buddha, could you have made a mistake?"

I said, "No, I am sure. This dog spirit only recently attached itself to him. It is not making any moves now, but it might in the future."

Pan Qing said, "We'll continue with our meal. After that, I will have a private word with Living Buddha Lian-sheng, Sheng-yen Lu. I don't want this to affect everybody."

After the dinner, Pan Qing invited me to another room. He was all serious when he said, "You're right on target!" Pan Qing then said, "I kept a German Shepherd dog at home. He was usually very loyal and adorable. But during the past few months the dog kept barking for no reason. He barked during the day and barked at night. It disturbed us and our neighbors. Our neighbors could not stand it and constantly complained. Despite our attempts to discipline him, he simply ignored us. We hit him and still he kept barking. We could not think of what else to try and finally we felt that the dog must have gone mad. We wanted to give him away, but who would want to keep a crazy dog? If we abandon him somewhere, we felt we would be irresponsible. Finally, I decided to mix an insecticide called Parathion into his dog food and silenced him for good."

I nodded my head after listening to his story. Pan Qing asked me, "Now that the dog has attached its spirit to me, what will it do?"

"I'm not sure myself."

"Will it stay for a while and then leave?"

"It's possible."

"I wish this is the case." Pan Qing said.

"That would be great!"

* * *

In a situation like this where a dog spirit attached itself to a person, I would not offer to help out if Pan Qing did not ask me to drive away the dog spirit. Moreover, Pan Qing was fine and there was nothing wrong with him. He was not particularly worried and I said no more.

About three months later, Cao Zong came to me and said, "Pan Qing is dead."

"How did he die?" I was astonished.

"Acute hepatitis. We sent him to the hospital but they couldn't save him."

"Oh my goodness! It happened so soon!"

Cao Zong told me, "After Pang Qing died, a strange phenomenon began to happen in his house. Pan Qing's family was terrified and now they would like to request you to help them."

"What kind of strange phenomenon is happening?"

Cao Zong said, "Mrs. Pan is having recurring dreams of Pan Qing telling her to seek your help. If not, everyone will be in danger. The strange phenomenon involves a pungent smell in the house which is unbearable. It smells like a stray dog that has not had a good bath for a long time. The lingering smell simply won't disperse. One after another, the family members have fallen ill. Mrs. Pan's body is swelling all over, and her skin is dried up and cracked. Pan Jing, the younger daughter, has been suffering from headaches. The elder son Pan Ming is even weirder, as his eyes have turned quite reddish, just like a rabid dog's eyes. This occurred after Pan Qing's death. Pan Ming's behavior also went through a transformation. He became irritable and depressed, always pacing around the house and appearing very sad. The most interesting thing is that objects in the house seem to move around by themselves. Clothing placed at one spot is found at another. A shower cap from the bathroom appears on the sofa mysteriously. Books on the shelf fall onto the floor all at once, not just one or two at a time. Trash collected is scattered all over the place. The kitchen is unoccupied, yet the forks and knifes, pots and pans rattle. At night, when everyone goes to sleep, you hear noises in the house, as if someone is walking around. In addition, there's the sound of knocking on walls as well."

Cao Zong said all of this without stopping. I said, "Let's go over to the house!"

Pan Qing had lived in a luxurious residence at a villa in the suburbs. The entrance led to a small fountain decorated with a small mountain and an artificial garden. The living room was spacious and the floor was tiled with marble. The windows were adorned with decorative artwork and the furniture was exquisite and tasteful.

Pan Qing was in charge of a major trading firm. Hence, he enjoyed a good life. Mrs. Pan and the two kids were present and I examined Pan Ming. Pan Ming's eyes were reddish and despite taking the doctor's prescribed medicine, the conjunctivitis, or pink eye, simply would not go away. This was because the dog spirit was attached to Pan Ming's body.

I said, "The dog spirit is on Pan Ming."

Pan Ming said nothing, stood up and stared fiercely at me. The family was horrified. I said, "Don't worry. I can deal with this."

Pan Ming then said, "I have an urge to charge forward and bite Living Buddha Lu, but I am suppressing it."

"Don't worry, I can handle it."

"Living Buddha, you must drive out this spirit!" Mrs. Pan said.

"There's no need for exorcism!" I said, "All I need to do is to sit in meditation on the living room floor for a while. Please be quiet." I sat down on the marble floor in the lotus position [or padmasana] and formed the Meditation Mudra [also called the Dharma Realm Samadhi Mudra]. I sat with my spine straightened and shoulders spread. I then tilted my head forward, bending the neck downwards to press my chin against my Adam's apple. My tongue touched the palate and my eyes were still and focused. Seated in stillness, I cleared my thoughts and balanced my body and mind.

I chanted:

> **[transliteration:] Om, si-ba-wa, su-da, sa-er-wa, da-er-ma, si-ba-wa, su-do, hang** (three times)
> **[Sanskrit: OM SOBHAWA SHUDDHA SARVA DHARMA SOBHAWA SHUDDHO HAM]** (this is the Emptiness Visualization Mantra).

With the power of blessing from the buddhas, the dharma realm, and my own cultivation power combined, I was transformed into emptiness.

The dog spirit could not see me. I silently chanted:

> **[transliteration:] Namo, sa-wa-dan-ta-ye-dou, wa-lu-zhi-di, om, san-bo-la, san-bo-la, hum** (three times)
> **[Sanskrit: NAMAH SARVA TATHAGATA-AVALOKITE OM SAM-BHARA SAM-BHARA HUM]** (this is the Food Transformation Mantra).

I was transformed into a pile of bones. Having been transformed into a pile of tasty bones, the dog spirit would certainly be most enticed when he saw me. The dog spirit jumped and bit the bones, and thus entered my body. With this, the dog spirit left Pan Ming's body and attached itself to me.

I stood up and announced to Pan Qing's family, "The dog spirit is now on my body. I am taking him away. From now on, your household will be peaceful and everything will be fine."

This was what I said and the life of Pan's family indeed returned to normal.

When I left the Pan family's home, the strange smell of a stray dog that has not taken a bath, whose skin was rotting, simply disappeared.

Mrs. Pan's swollen body and dry skin recovered from that day onwards. She had to urinate a lot, but then the swelling subsided completely. Her dry and cracking skin also improved greatly, and within three days, all illnesses were cured. Mrs. Pan found it to be a miracle, as she recovered without taking any medication.

Pan Qing's daughter's headache went away, as if someone had taken a rock off of her head; she felt much better. Pan Ming's reddened and inflamed eyes, much like those of a rabid dog, were healed. His behavior showed a marked recovery and he was once again a healthy and fine young man.

The strange phenomena in the house also ceased. Objects were no longer showing up in different places, and there were no more strange noises. The Pan family was very grateful for my help.

Now the problem was not at the Pan family residence, but was instead on my body. I realized that this German Shepherd's spirit has a great deal of spiritual power. It was dashing all over my body, wanting to break out. I was not ready to release him. My body was like an iron cage, locking it within me; there was no escape. Having lost its freedom, it would not be able to harm anyone.

The dog spirit told me, "I will bite your liver!"

I knew Pan Qing was bitten to death this way. I said, "Go ahead and bite!" The dog bit and broke his canine teeth, as I had transformed my liver into a vajra.

"I will bite your heart!" The dog proceeded, yet I transformed my heart into stainless steel.

"I will bite your intestines," and the dog bit me. My intestines had been turned into a piece of granite. The dog barked and said, "Your heart is stone cold!" I laughed out loud.

Although this dog spirit could do no harm to me, its filthy energy was having an effect on me and was polluting my body.

I chanted the Pure Water Mantra:

The genuine water of the Primordial,
Its liquid crystal clear,
Purify the spirit and let wisdom grow,
Nurturing all living beings so they may flourish,

Cleansing and purifying everything far and near,
Through cultivation one advances towards the Jade Capital.

[Pronunciation of original Taoist text: Wu ji zhen shui, ye ti xian ming, jing xi ling tai zhi hui sheng, wan wu zi run rong, xia er cheng qing, xiu dao shang yu jing.]

I chanted the Mind Purification Mantra:

My spirit is genuine as I cultivate purely.
My mind is genuine as I cultivate purely.
My qi is genuine as I cultivate purely.
My five organs are genuinely purified.

[Pronunciation of original Taoist text: Shen cheng jing xiu, yi cheng jing xiu, qi cheng jing xiu, wu zang cheng jing.]

I recited the Speech Purification Mantra:

My throat is cleansed as I cultivate purely.
My tongue is cleansed as I cultivate purely.
My teeth are cleansed as I cultivate purely.
My three karmas are cleansed and purified.

[Pronunciation of original Taoist text: Hou qing jing xiu, she qing jing xiu, chi qing jing xiu, san ye qing jing.]

I chanted the Body Purification Mantra:

My body is clean as I cultivate purely.
I am cleansed as I cultivate purely.
I am neat as I cultivate purely.
My heart is clean and pure.

[Pronunciation of original Taoist text: Ti jie jing xiu, qing jie jing xiu, zheng jie jing xiu, yi xin jie jing.]

I recited the Three Karmas Purification Mantra:

The realms that exist within one's body,
All thirty-six thousand spirits,
Fulfill your duties within the organs.
From the past to the future,
May I enjoy good health,
May I always dwell in the Three Treasures.
When met with destruction,
My body will remain forever,
As I recite this True Scripture,
The karmas of body, speech and mind are purified.
Execute this order at once.

[Pronunciation of original Taoist text: Shen zhong zhu nei jing, san wan liu qian shen, dong zuo lu xing zang, qian jie bing hou ye, yuan wo shen zi zai, chang zhu san bao zhong, dang yu jie huai shi, wo shen chang bu mie, song ci zhen wen shi, sheng xin kou ye jie qing jing, ji ji ru lu ling.]

When I finished my recitation, my body and mind became purified of the filthy energy. Remarkably, upon listening to my mantra recitation, the dog spirit became purified in its body and mind. It listened quietly. I was happy that the karma of the dog spirit was cleansed at the end of my chanting.

Finally, I chanted the Heaven and Earth Purification Mantra:

Heaven and earth are balanced with nature.

All pollution will disperse.
The mystical wonders within the heavenly zone.
The illuminating Supreme Origin, Tai Yuan.
The powerful gods of the Eight Directions.
Let me become one with nature.
Talisman Mandate of the Numinous Treasure, Ling Bao,
Announcing to the Nine Heavens.
Qian Lou Da Na.
Energy Wind from the Heavenly Zone of Supreme Mystery,
Sever demons and bind evil.
Kill tens of thousands of ghosts.
This Central Mountain Magical Mantra.
The Jade Scripture of the Primordial, Yuan Shi.
Recite this once,
Curing all sicknesses and prolonging life.
Circulate this order in the Five Mountains,
Throughout all Eight Seas it will be known.
The Demon King will be defeated.
Guard me at my residence.
All filth and pollution will be eliminated.
The Tao Qi will always prosper.
Execute this order at once.

[Pronunciation of original Taoist text: Tian di zi ran, hui qi fen san, dong zhong xuan xu, huang lang tai yuan, ba fang wei shen, shi wo si ran, ling bao fu ming, pu gao jiu tian, qian luo da na, dong gang tai xuan, zhan yao fu xie, sha gui wan qian, zhong shan shen zhou, yuan shi yu wen, chi song yi bian, que bing yan nian, an xing wu yue, ba hai zhi wen, mo wang shu shou, shi wei wo xuan, xiong hui dang jin, dao qi chang cun, ji ji ru lu ling.]

Upon reciting this mantra, the dog spirit shrunk to half of its size and became immobilized. It was tied up. The dog spirit yelled, "Stop chanting. Stop chanting. I am willing to take refuge!"

"You want to take refuge. That's good," I said.

This dog spirit was rather clever. If it did not take refuge with the Buddha, all I needed was to chant the Heaven and Earth Purification Mantra three more times and its spirit would shrink to an even smaller size, or disintegrate in a loud thunderclap.

The dog spirit screamed, "Let me go and I will take refuge!"

Of course I would let it out. Since the dog spirit was attached to me, the fact that it would be taking refuge meant that I would be taking refuge as well.

As I emptied my body and mind, the dog spirit was finally freed. At the moment of release, the cunning dog spirit wanted to escape. Its request to take refuge was only a trick.

Dog spirits or animal entities usually have minor psychic powers. As it leaped into the sky to escape, a god appeared and hit the dog, which then fell to the ground. Then it attempted to disappear underground but was stopped by another god. It dashed towards the left and there stood another god. It dashed towards the right and there stood yet another god. The dog spirit cried out, "That's it! That's it! You have me surrounded and I can't escape. I must really take refuge with you."

The dog spirit lay on the ground and expressed its desire to take refuge. I laughed heartily and said, "You dog demon. You must be taught a good lesson before you would learn to be good. I am well aware of this. Thus, I have secretly chanted the Taoist Earth Deity Mantra:

Under the guardianship of the Primeval Lord,
Notify all spirits,
Genuine sovereigns of the mountains and rivers,
Land and local gods,
Earth and grain gods on the altar,

Do not create disturbances.
Return to the right path,
Be purified inwardly and outwardly,
And stationed in one's rightful place,
Be prepared to guard over the shrine.
The Supreme One issues an edict.
To capture the demons.
The dharma protector deities,
Guard over one's sutra recitation.
Take refuge in the Tao,
And all will prosper and be well.
Execute this order at once.

[Pronunciation of original Taoist text: Yuan shi an zhen, pu gao wan ling, yue du zhen guan, tu di zhi shen, zuo she you ji, bu de wan jing, hui xiang zheng dao, nei wai cheng qing, ge an fang wei, bei shou tan ting, tai shang you ming, sou bu xie jing, hu fa shen wang, bao wei song jing, gui yi da dao, yuan heng li zhen, ji ji ru lu ling.]

The dog spirit remained still, not daring to make a move. I gave the dog spirit the Fourfold Refuge:

I take refuge in the Vajra Guru. Namo Guru bei.
I take refuge in the Buddha. Namo Buddha ye.
I take refuge in the Dharma. Namo Dharma ye.
I take refuge in the Sangha. Namo Sangha ye.

I recited the Fourfold Refuge Mantra. This mantra can turn a polluted ground into a pure land.

([transliteration:] Om pu kan
[Sanskrit: OM BHUH KHAM].)

The dog spirit willingly accepted. I had planned to send the dog spirit to the Western Paradise of Ultimate Bliss [Sukhavati, the Pure Land of Amitabha Buddha]. However, it had killed Pan Qing and remained cunning and shrewd. If I sent it to Sukhavati immediately, I felt it would be letting this dog off too easily. It would be difficult to imagine the victim still remaining in the netherworld while the dog spirit ascended to the Western Paradise, thus contradicting right and wrong. That would certainly be unfair.

What about sending the dog to hell? That would not be a good solution either. For some reason this dog spirit had come upon a vajra guru who gave it the Fourfold Refuge. With the transmission of the Fourfold Refuge and mantra, the dog spirit gained an affinity with the Buddha. If it was sent to hell, I was afraid it would be difficult for the dog spirit to get out, and hell is certainly not a place for cultivation. I found myself with a dilemma.

Then an earth deity came and put a leash on the dog and said, "Don't worry, Living Buddha. I'll take care of this!"

I was overjoyed and said, "This is great! You are taking this dog to guard the temple. This dog can guard the temple altar!"

The earth deity waved and said, "You won't have to worry about this anymore."

Here is a verse:

Throughout heaven and earth lies the law
The Buddhas in all compassion transmit the heart teachings
If one takes refuge and obtains mantras
One will return to find purity upon the other shore

9 This is What Shakyamuni Tathagata Expounds

A businessman by the name of Gu Quan had contracted stomach cancer. He searched everywhere for a cure, but his condition showed no signs of improvement. His illness became more severe and neither Western nor Chinese doctors could do much about it. On the other hand, his belief in secret remedies led him to spend a considerable amount of money on purchasing such prescriptions, but they were also ineffective.

Gu Quan was so desperate that he decided to approach a deity at a temple and said, "If I am cured of my cancer, I'll vow to build a temple and serve in the temple as an attendant for the rest of my life."

The deity replied, "You will recover."

Gu Quan asked, "Which deity can cure my cancer?"

The deity answered, "Shakyamuni Buddha."

"How can I find Shakyamuni Buddha? Where does he stay?"

"Go look for him at a Buddhist temple."

Gu Quan had never stepped into a monastery in his life. Thus, when he arrived at a Buddhist temple and asked where he could find Shakyamuni Buddha, the monk told him that the Buddha was in the Great Hall. When Gu Quan stepped into the Great Hall, he saw the golden statue of Shakyamuni Buddha seated in the middle of the hall. He bowed to the Buddha and made his promise, but the Buddha remained still and did not treat his condition at all.

Gu Quan became frantic, and asked a monk, "Can the Buddha cure illnesses?"

"If you're sincere, things can happen."

"Where can I find this Shakyamuni Buddha who can cure illness?"

The monk wanted to laugh, but held his laughter and replied, "If you're sincere, things can happen."

Gu Quan then asked, "I want to look for Shakyamuni Buddha to cure my illness. Where can I find him?"

The monk replied with a verse, "Do not go a long distance to seek the Buddha who resides in the spiritual mountain. The spiritual mountain actually lies within your heart."

"In the heart?" Gu Quan did not understand.

The monk became impatient with Gu Quan's persistent questioning and finally told him, "Go talk to Sheng-yen Lu."

"Why should I talk to Sheng-yen Lu?"

"Because..." the monk started and said, "Because Sheng-yen Lu and Shakyamuni Buddha always enjoy having coffee together."

This monk had read my books and he remembered my story of how I had coffee with the Buddha at a coffee shop.

Gu Quan was thrilled to learn of this and exclaimed, "I want to have coffee with Shakyamuni Buddha!"

The monk hurried him along and said, "Go quickly. Hurry up. Get a meeting with Sheng-yen Lu!"

Gu Quan came to see me. I told him that Shakyamuni Buddha was actually the son of King Suddhodana, ruler of Kapilavastu, and his mother was Queen Maya. He was born in the Lumbini Park, east of Kapilavastu, and was named Siddhartha.

In his youth, the Buddha contemplated the grim nature of life, such as hardships faced by the farmers, the sight of animals killing each other for food, and loathed the hostilities of life.

Once while traveling through the city, he witnessed the phenomenon of birth, old age, sickness and death. Thus, the Buddha, in his renunciation, became a monk. For six years he trained using ascetic practices and later realized that such austerities were not the way to enlightenment. He later bathed in the Nairanjana River and accepted the offering of milk-rice from a village girl.

Finally, he sat in meditation under the Bodhi tree, contemplated on the Four Noble Truths and the Twelve Links of Dependent Origination, and became the Enlightened World Honored One, teacher of gods and men.

After his enlightenment, the Buddha traveled to many places and preached to many groups of beings for over forty years. In the year 487 B.C., the Buddha entered nirvana under the two sala trees near the city of Kushinagar.

I briefly recounted the life of the Buddha and upon listening to my narration, Gu Quan finally understood. Gu Quan said, "I asked the deity and the deity said my cancer will recover if I can find Shakyamuni Buddha to cure my illness. Now that I understand Shakyamuni Buddha's life story, it appears that my cancer is incurable."

I told Gu Quan, "That's not the case!"

"You mean you have a secret remedy?"

"It's not that. You need to have faith when you fight cancer, and there are numerous cases of cancer patients who have survived the ordeal. You can believe in the Buddha and learn from his teachings. You can find liberation through them."

"This is how Shakyamuni Buddha heals?"

"That's right."

Gu Quan was very inquisitive and asked, "The Buddha died more than two thousand five hundred years ago. How is it possible that you can drink coffee with Shakyamuni Buddha?"

I asked him, "Do you believe it?"

"I believe it."

"Since you trust me, I will explain this to you clearly. The truth is actually quite simple. Although the Buddha entered into nirvana, his spiritual light extends across the universe. This is similar to Avalokitesvara Bodhisattva, who can answer a thousand prayers and appear simultaneously in a thousand places. The Buddha ranks higher than the Bodhisattva and thus can do likewise. I, Living Buddha Liansheng, Sheng-yen Lu have cultivated the spiritual light and I can certainly meet the Buddha and drink coffee with him in our spiritual light bodies. This is spirit meeting spirit, and is actually a very natural thing."

I said, "Besides this, when a person passes away, his body may be no more, but his spirit remains. When another person dies, these two spirits can meet each other. What I mean is that the difference between life and death is simply that in life, there is a physical body, and in death, there is no physical body. Life and death is thus one reality. In birth one refers to existence in the human world and in death one refers to existence in the netherworld."

I continued, "I can leave my body with my spirit. As long as I stay concentrated, seated in the lotus position, circulate the qi, channel, light drop and light, and move my spirit out of the body, I can enter the dharma realm and meet Shakyamuni Buddha himself!"

Gu Quan listened but did not fully comprehend what I had said. He asked, "Since you can meet up with Shakyamuni Buddha, can you do me a favor and ask the Buddha how cancer can be cured?"

"Oh!" I paused and thought about this before I replied, "To meet the Buddha depends on circumstances and affinity. It happens naturally."

"No matter what you must help me!"

"All right!" I nodded my head and said, "But you have to listen to my instructions. You need to enshrine a statue of Shakyamuni Buddha, recite one sutra, and chant Shakyamuni Buddha's name with focus and perseverance. Can you do this?"

"Yes!"

Gu Quan displayed the utmost sincerity as he enshrined the statue of Shakyamuni Buddha. I taught him how to recite the *High King Avalokitesvara Sutra* and to recite the Buddha's name.

Gu Quan believes the verses outlined in the *High King Sutra,* "One is liberated from the suffering of birth and death, and freed from all the many kinds of suffering." Gu Quan was even more devoted and sincere in his recitation of the sutra and the Buddha's name because of his illness.

This is:

In reciting any sutra one should persist all the way
Ceasing all thoughts if you may
In the Saha world's ocean of suffering one will see
The wind and wave is as calm as it can be
Thus riding in a boat towards the Lotus Land
One sails steadily

* * *

One night, I had a strange dream. I found myself walking alone on a small road. As I was walking, I suddenly heard the cries of many people. A group of people, both young and old, about a hundred of them, were running towards me. They looked like they were running from some calamity.

I asked, "What's happening?"

One of them said, "Some robbers entered our village and started killing people and we escaped!"

"Who is the leader of the robbers?"

"Gu Quan," the person replied.

While in the dream, I realized Gu Quan's cancer was a result of his past karma. He had killed too many people and the resentment crystallized as cancer. Gu Quan's karma was heavy and it was no easy task to save him. I felt very dejected and in deep sorrow I broke down and cried.

As I was grief-stricken, I heard a voice from the sky, "Lian-sheng, why are you so sad?"

I replied, "Gu Quan!"

When I replied, I looked up the sky and saw Avalokitesvara Bodhisattva. The Bodhisattva was smiling and her hand held a vase with a willow stem. She turned the vase and said, "Lian-sheng, look!"

Out of the vase emitted a white light. This white light is one of magnificence and wonder, complete in all merits and shows wondrous equanimity towards all. It is inconceivably limitless in its scope and yet it can change with the flow and strength of the wind. It can overcome the three lower realms [of animals, hungry ghosts, and hell].

Within the white light appeared men, women, young and old, a mix of all kinds of people. I was amazed at the sight. Avalokitesvara Bodhisattva said, "These are the spirits of those killed by Gu Quan. Now I am leading them away. In the future, these spirits will become lotus born manifestations from Amitabha Buddha's pure consciousness. They share the same world and there will be no other."

I was overjoyed and said, "So the Bodhisattva has liberated all those killed by Gu Quan?"

"That's right."

Avalokitesvara Bodhisattva added, "When I was at the Maha Thunder Monastery, Shakyamuni Buddha instructed me that if I meet Lian-sheng, I need to teach you a mantra so that you can in turn impart it to Gu Quan. This mantra will purify Gu Quan and set his body and mind at ease, eradicating the cancerous tumor completely."

"What is the mantra?"

Avalokitesvara Bodhisattva then recited the divine mantra:

[transliteration:] Da-zhi-ta, er-lan-di, er-lan-mi, shi-li-bei, shi-

li-shi-li, mo-jie-shi-zhi, san-po-ba-dou, so-ha
[Sanskrit: TADYATHA ALANTE ALANME SRIBI SRI SRI MAKASIJI SAMBHAVATU SVAHA].

I memorized the divine mantra and held my palms in respect and saw Avalokitesvara Bodhisattva off. The Bodhisattva gradually left on auspicious clouds.

I taught Gu Quan the divine mantra. He was very hardworking and recited it day and night.

Gu Quan went for a medical check-up after two months and found out his stomach cancer had miraculously disappeared. The count of cancerous cells was zero. Gu Quan had made a full recovery and this sent him jumping for joy.

I was happy for him. This is:

Reciting mantra leaves no room for erroneous thoughts
Every sound of chanting thus flows from within the heart
Purifying all the way
The rootless cancerous tumor will disperse naturally

Later, I came across *The Sutra of Curing Malignant Tumors and Hemorrhoids* in the Buddhist Canon and realized the similarities between the mantra from the sutra and the one transmitted by Shakyamuni Buddha himself. I was amazed to find out that the so-called piles as described in this sutra refer not only to hemorrhoids, but also refer to tumors and cancer. If you read the text of the sutra you will know what I mean.

I am including the sutra here:

The Sutra of Curing Malignant Tumors and Hemorrhoids

Thus have I heard. At one time the Buddha was in the Bam-

boo Grove in the city of Rajagriha, accompanied by five hundred monks. Many monks were suffering from malignancies and hemorrhoids and as a result they had become thin and weak. Tormented day and night by these diseases, the monks lived in constant pain and agony. The Venerable Ananda observed the situation and went to the place where the Buddha was. Bowing his head in obeisance before the feet of the Buddha, Ananda stood up and said to the Buddha, "World-Honored One, there are many monks residing in Rajagriha who are suffering from cancerous diseases and as a result have become thin and weak. They are living in constant pain and are tormented by these diseases day and night. World-Honored One, is there a way to cure these diseases?"

The Buddha said to Ananda, "Listen to this *Sutra of Curing Malignant Tumors and Hemorrhoids.* Read and recite it, accept and uphold it. Memorize it well and propagate it far and wide. These tumors and hemorrhoids will be removed. Tumors formed from internal wind, heat [disorder], blood disorder, combination of wind, heat and blood disorder, bleeding hemorrhoids, stomach cancer, nasal cavity and paranasal sinus cancer, oral cancer, tongue cancer, eye cancer, ear cancer, head cancer, arm and feet tumor, spinal cord cancer, rectal tumor and hemorrhoid, tumors or sarcomas arising from the skeletal and connective tissues.

Such tumors will fall off upon drying and thus be eliminated. All diseases will be cured. Thus, recite this divine mantra. The mantra is:

[transliteration:] Da-zhi-ta, er-lan-di, er-lan-mi, shi-li-bei, shi-li-shi-li, mo-jie-shi-zhi, san-po-ba-dou, so-ha
[Sanskrit: TADYATHA ALANTE ALANME SRIBI SRI SRI MAKASIJI SAMBHAVATU SVAHA].

Ananda! To the North of here, there is a huge snow mountain

where this Phalasa tree called Sudurjaya (Difficult to Conquer) grows. It has three types of flowers. One is early bloom, the second, full bloom, and third, wrinkled. Likewise, the monks' illnesses will dry up and fall off like the flowers. The bleeding will stop and you will find no pus. The monks' suffering and pain will be eliminated and they will recover completely. This is due to the action of drying up the tumors.

If you recite this sutra constantly, you will gain the knowledge of recollecting seven of your past lives, thus achieving attainment of the mantra. Soha. Thus, another mantra:

> **[transliteration:] Da-zhi-ta, zhan-mi-zhan-mi, she-zhan-ni, she-mo-ni, she-zhan-ni, so-ha**
> **[Sanskrit: TADYATHA JARMI JARMI SERJAMI SERMANI SERJANI SVAHA]."**

When the Buddha had finished expounding this sutra, Ananda and the other members of the assembly were filled with joy, and they believed and accepted it and respectfully put it into practice.

* * *

I personally feel that illness ranks first among the sufferings in this Saha or human world. The Buddhist sutras mention that arising from the four elements of earth, water, fire and wind are four hundred and four kinds of illnesses. Every illness is tormenting and painful, especially cancer, as it remains incurable even today.

Shakyamuni Buddha's mantra on curing cancer is:

> **[transliteration:] Da-zhi-ta, er-lan-di, er-lan-mi, shi-li-bei, shi-li-shi-li, mo-jie-shi-zhi, san-po-ba-dou, so-ha**
> **[Sanskrit: TADYATHA ALANTE ALANME SRIBI SRI SRI MAKASIJI SAMBHAVATU SVAHA].**

This mantra is rarely seen and not many are aware of it. It is recorded in the Chinese Buddhist Canon [Zhonghua Dazangjing], first series, volume five, on page 16868. This mantra has helped many people!

I know of another case. A person by the name of He Cai approached me. He knelt at my front door and despite my attempts to lift him up, he simply refused to stand up. He would not get up unless I promised to save him. I finally gave in, and he stood up.

I asked him, "What's wrong?"

"I have cancer, in the last stage."

"What type of cancer?"

"Hodgkin's lymphoma in the armpits." He Cai pull up his sleeves and showed me. I was taken aback at the sight of lymph nodes spreading over the skin. The malignant tumor cells had spread to the bones and other areas. I shook my head as I knew he was beyond any treatment. I asked, "What did the doctors say?"

He Cai replied, "They said I would die within half a year."

I told He Cai I would do my best to help him, but I could only do so much. He had to seek help from Shakyamuni Buddha himself!

I taught him the Cancer Curing Mantra of Shakyamuni Buddha. I mentioned that after chanting the mantra, he would need to recite these lines of blessing, "I am disciple He Cai, presently suffering from cancer. I pray to the Buddha for your blessing. May you bestow your compassion upon me so that my cancerous disease may be removed and my life prolonged. Namo Shakyamuni Buddha. Namo the Buddhas of the Ten Directions. Namo the Dharma of the Ten Directions. Namo the Sangha of the Ten Directions."

Upon returning home, He Cai did as he was instructed. After twenty-one days of cultivation, while in a twilight state between waking and sleeping, he saw Shakyamuni Buddha appearing before him. Shakyamuni Buddha spoke to him, "He Cai, your illness is incurable.

Leave this world with me!"

"No! I want to live!"

"The human world is an ocean of suffering. It is a mansion in flames. Isn't it better to leave with me?"

"No! My wish is not fulfilled. I have to stay alive!" He Cai insisted.

"How many more years do you need to fulfill this wish of yours?"

"Five years."

Shakyamuni Buddha said, "Very well then. You will have five more years. You should continue chanting this mantra."

Interestingly, after having this dream, He Cai's illness was somewhat alleviated. He felt like he was normal and his health was like that of an average person. The cancer was not eradicated, but it had not worsened, and it spread no further temporarily. He Cai lived another five years, and when the time came, his tumor spread and he passed away.

He Cai's cancer was not cured, but it did not become more malignant, thus allowing him to fulfill his wish before he died. Regarding He Cai's case, I feel it had little to do with the effectiveness of the Cancer Curing Mantra, but rather, his time was up. Not even the Buddha could save his life. If his life could have been saved, then nobody on earth would die. However, I discovered this Cancer Curing Mantra can prolong one's life, and I believe it can deliver one to the Buddha's Pure Land, thus explaining why Shakyamuni Buddha himself would appear and receive He Cai upon his death!

Reciting mantra leaves no room for erroneous thoughts
Every sound of chanting thus flows from within the heart
Purifying all the way
The rootless cancerous tumor will disperse naturally

Sheng-yen Lu

10 A Fulfilled Vow

A lay Buddhist by the name of Li Wei had taken refuge with Master Kuang-chin [a Chinese Buddhist monk and master]. His mother, Mrs. Huang, was also a disciple of his. Mrs. Huang passed away one year following the death of the senior monk. Throughout her life she had devoted herself to charity, alms-giving, as well as Buddhism.

One time, Li Wei took part in a pilgrimage up a mountain. This pilgrimage involved a group of pilgrims bowing once every three steps from the foot of the mountain towards the Great Hall of the temple situated at the top of the mountain. Everyone was chanting the Buddha's name, and leading the group was a community of monks holding an instrument called a liu-yin [a handheld brass gong attached to a wooden handle and stringed to a striker]. The liu-yin is a ritual instrument which produces a chiming sound when struck. Everyone listens to the sound as it signals all to kneel or bow, walk or chant the Buddha's name.

The constant flow of pilgrims formed a long and winding crowd of people, adorning the place with liveliness and a sacred atmosphere. Going on a pilgrimage has its advantages:

1. Climbing mountains is good exercise.
2. Cultivation through sincere prostration.
3. Recitation of the Buddha's name.
4. Cessation of erroneous thoughts.

Taking a pilgrimage on this rather rugged mountain was a test for every pilgrim, as the rugged dirt pathway wound up a few thousand feet. Li Wei followed the contingent of pilgrims, chanting the Buddha's name and bowing sincerely. He once turned his head and saw a group of women in the pilgrimage. Among them was a woman who was carrying an incense bag. She looked just like his mother.

Li Wei was stunned. He waved at her and she waved back. Li Wei was sure that the woman was his mother. He quickly left his group and hurried towards the woman. Yet when he looked again, the woman who looked just like his mother was gone. Li Wei could not believe his eyes, but she was nowhere to be seen. Li Wei trusted his eyes and knew the woman was his mother. He had no doubt about that, yet she had simply disappeared.

Most people thought Li Wei was seeing things. Li Wei said, "My mother was really among the group of women and we waved to each other. How could she have disappeared within the few steps that I took towards her? What is happening here?"

Outsiders felt it was simply impossible. When someone has passed away, that person cannot possibly come back to life. He must have been seeing things. A debate resulted between two camps. Someone suggested to Li Wei, "You should talk to Living Buddha Lian-sheng, Sheng-yen Lu."

"Why go to him?" Li Wei asked.

"He has spiritual abilities," the person replied.

* * *

Li Wei came to me and said, “Please tell me the truth of the matter!”

I asked the buddhas and bodhisattvas for an answer, and they gave me a verse in reply:

Keeping a strong and determined vow
And carrying a marvelous bag of incense
One praises the merits of the buddhas
And displays a countenance of compassion

I told Li Wei, “Your mother has a round face with long and thin eyebrows and a pair of compassionate eyes. Her teeth have a special feature - one of her front teeth was a gold tooth that slanted to the right. It was on the bottom row of her teeth.”

Li Wei exclaimed, “That’s absolutely correct! You even got the features of her teeth right. This is simply incredible. Master, may I ask what the significance of my mother’s appearance is?”

I replied, “Your mother has an unfulfilled vow.”

“What vow?”

I replied, “When your mother was alive, she loved charity work and had volunteered to serve in a monastery for many years. She once made a vow to the buddhas and bodhisattvas that she wanted to build this pilgrimage road on the mountain. However, the cost and budget of this work was huge and she did not have the means to accomplish the task. Soon after she had made this vow she passed away. Thus, this vow of hers remained unfulfilled. Thus, it was possible that when she appeared to you during the pilgrimage, she was hoping that you might help her fulfill this vow of paving and building this pilgrimage road.”

Li Wei told me his mother had indeed served as a volunteer for many years with the monastery and was very charitable. She had donated almost all the money that her husband and her children gave her to charity. However, he had not heard of his mother’s vow to construct the road for the pilgrimage. Li Wei decided to ask his father about this matter; perhaps he would know about it.

Li Wei went to ask his father. His father confirmed there was such a vow, but because of his less than ideal financial situation, he could not carry out the vow.

Li Wei returned to tell me, "Grand Master Lu! Your divination is truly remarkable. Besides knowing about the human world, you're able to know the things of the netherworld. This is simply unbelievable!"

"Why don't you fulfill your mother's vow?" I said.

Li Wei said, "It's not that I don't want to do it. I am more than willing to carry out this task, but the circumstances are not right."

"What circumstances?"

"I don't have the money."

I said, "I'll teach you a mantra and you will have money!"

Li Wei smiled and said, "Grand Master Lu, you must be joking."

"No, I am serious," I told him. "I am willing to teach you this mantra because your mother had made a vow to build this road of pilgrimage and you're carrying out this vow for her. If you chant this mantra you will have great fortune within a few years. Remember, once you're rich, you must fulfill this vow."

Li Wei asked, "Such a mantra really exists?"

I said, "Certainly."

I took out a sutra. It was the *Vasudhara Dharani Sutra*. The sutra states:

> **"If any good man should write and accept this sutra, he will receive all joy and enjoy peace and prosperity. If anyone should adopt vegetarianism and celibacy, and recite daily, he will receive great wealth and prestige."**

Li Wei was apprehensive and said, "To adopt vegetarianism and celibacy?"

I said, "How about this. Don't feel anxious. I keep my methods natural and simple. I don't want you to stick to vegetarianism and adopt a pure lifestyle. As long as you recite OM AH HUM once before a meal and once before you make love, you can continue as usual."

In addition, I taught him, "When you recite this mantra, you must first recite it eight hundred times. After that, you will recite it three times a day: once in the morning, once in the afternoon and once at night, one hundred and eight recitations each time."

"Is the mantra long?"

"It's only a few syllables long. It's very simple."

I wrote the mantra for him:

[transliteration:] Om, va-su, da-li, so-ha
[Sanskrit: OM VASU DHARE SVAHA].

Li Wei read it and said, "That's simple enough. I can do it."

I told Li Wei, "Don't underestimate the three syllables OM AH HUM. These three syllables are the Three Syllables of Vidya. Vidya is purity, also described as a transformation into purity; hence, pure living. These three syllables are beyond comprehension, carrying a meaning that is deep and profound. Thus, they are simply unfathomable."

"The Vasudhara Dharani can certainly attract great wealth and prestige. This mantra is not widely known, and is very precious. I don't transmit it lightly. I only teach it to those who truly keep their vows."

"Does it require empowerment?"

"Yes. All mantras of Vajrayana require empowerment so that the power of the lineage transmission is linked."

I gave Li Wei the empowerment. Here is a verse:

Vegetarianism and pure living are required

But most people simply cannot do it
One who stirs no dust in life is already a buddha
Thus there is nothing bizarre about transforming into purity
Every layman is in reality a buddha
Yet men are obsessed with wealth and fortune
My transmission of a mantra today is done in the name of charity
An enlightened lotus must bloom in the face of a deluded heart

* * *

Li Wei trusted me, and he had faith in the Vasudhara Dharani Mantra. Li Wei was not new to Buddhism. He knew that to follow the Buddha's way, you need to make these five great vows:

Living beings are innumerable; I vow to liberate them all.
Blessings and wisdom are endless; I vow to gather them all.
Dharma methods are countless; I vow to learn them all.
The buddhas are supreme; I vow to serve them all.
The ways of bodhi are limitless; I vow to attain them all.
Everyone in the dharma realm will benefit from this.

Li Wei had always wanted to learn Buddhism, and he was devoted to his parents. He thus shared his mother's vow and felt that he should set out to complete whatever vow that his mother could not fulfill.

Every time he completed his chanting, he would dedicate the merits: "May the prayers of sentient beings, bearing such remarkable vows of this world and beyond, quickly be fulfilled."

Li Wei cultivated for a year. His financial state remained unchanged, and there was no response of any kind, but he persisted without losing hope. One night, he had an interesting dream. He dreamed of his mother taking him for a flight.

He asked his mother, "When will my financial situation improve?"

His mother replied, “The conditions are ripe!”

He then asked, “What about the vow to build the pilgrimage road. Will it remain unfulfilled?”

His mom replied, “The conditions are ripe!”

They flew to a hill and landed on the ground. The mother pointed to the hill and said, “Remember this. To the left of this place lies a small temple of an earth deity. To your right is a grave. In front there is a bridge over a stream and it is called Pu-li Bridge.”

“This hill?” Li Wei was skeptical.

“Purchase it.”

“But there's no value to this piece of barren hill!” Li Wei was in doubt.

Again his mother said, “Purchase it.”

Li Wei woke up from this dream and realized he was still lying in bed. But the conversation he had with his mother still lingered and the two words “purchase it” came through loud and clear.

One day, one of Li Wei's friends was having financial difficulties and he needed to sell his assets. He pleaded to Li Wei to purchase his land, and he was willing to sell it at a bargain.

His friend brought Li Wei to see a hill. To his astonishment, Li Wei saw that it was the same hill he had seen in his dream. There was an earth deity temple to the left and a grave to the right. In the middle was a bridge across a running stream.

Li Wei told his friend, “The bridge is named Pu-li.”

His friend said, “When I first purchased this place the bridge was already there. I have never paid attention to its name.”

They approached the bridge and checked. It was indeed named “Pu-li Bridge.” His friend was shocked and asked, “Have you been here before?”

Li Wei replied, “I have been here in a dream.”

The friend said, “You must be kidding me!”

Li Wei did as his mother had instructed in his dream and purchased the barren hill at a real bargain. After the purchase, Li Wei was confused as to what to do with it. Did his mother want him to grow fruits, such as lychees, longans, plums, papayas, bananas...?

People mocked Li Wei for being foolish. These days, there was simply no way a person could get rich by planting fruits. Li Wei also felt that he made a bad decision. Every now and then he would take a trip to the hill. He realized that this hill had little to offer. Even if he tried to grow fruits here, he did not have the expertise to do so. The development of residential communities amongst the hills had not yet expanded to the region where his hill was, so he won't be constructing residential buildings. He never planned to build a columbarium [a place where people's cremated remains are stored]. What about building a temple? But who would bother to build a temple in a remote hilly location? As for turning it into a cemetery, this hill also does not have good feng shui for a burial ground.

Li Wei just could not figure it out. Many had wondered about this. Li Wei's purchase of this hill was purely based on a dream. He told other people about it and they thought he had lost his mind.

However, Li Wei discovered cool and refreshing spring water flowing from a low-lying area in the hill since his purchase of the place. At first he didn't pay much attention to it. But as the water was gushing out continuously in great volume, flowing into the riverbank nearby, an idea struck Li Wei. He bottled a sample and sent it to a laboratory for testing. It turned out to be high quality natural mineral water. This water contained no fat, carbohydrates, or protein. It contains sodium, calcium, magnesium, iron, fluoride, etc. The laboratory report stated that the water was of superb quality and contained minerals needed and absorbed by the human body. It contained no deposits and tasted refreshingly cool. It was mineral water. Li Wei linked this idea to building a factory for mineral water. He came to me for a name, "Please give the mineral water a good brand name."

I first named it, "Simply Pure, Fresh, Crystal Clear."

Li Wei said, "That seems repetitive."

I gave it another name, "Pu-li."

Li Wei uttered, "That's it! It clicks!"

The name of the bridge was Pu-li Bridge. He named his hill Pu-li Hill, so it was only fitting to call the water that springs forth from the hill Pu-li Mineral Water!

When Pu-li Mineral Water was launched, its sales skyrocketed and were very well received. Pu-li Mineral Water swept the market and consumers simply loved it. It became the drink of choice over other brands of mineral water.

This is:

- Popular among people.
- Beneficial to all.

Even stranger was the fact that the spring water from the hill kept flowing, as if there was an inexhaustible underground river beneath the hill.

Li Wei did not forget his vow. Upon receiving his blessings, he quickly completed the pilgrimage road, and thus fulfilled his mother's vow. Li Wei, like his mother, gave to charity and as a wealthy man, he donated huge sums of money. Many Buddhist organizations approached him for donations.

Li Wei supported the building of temples, hospitals, etc. I saw Li Wei appear on television and receive praise for his charity.

One year, I returned to Taiwan. I went past a rather grand and luxurious building and asked, "Whose company is this?"

"Li Wei's."

I uttered "Ah!" and fell silent. I heard later that Li Wei was always trying to see me, but I did not see him. It was not until one time when he sent a car to pick me up that I finally visited his house. His house was guarded with a security sentry at the gate. The house appeared magnificent, a testimony to Li Wei's status as the chairman of many companies.

Li Wei came downstairs and when we met he appeared very warm and friendly. He told his servants to take good care of me. He said, "Why didn't you ever come to see me?"

I said, "Sorry! I am really busy!"

"What are you busy with?"

"I'm busy liberating sentient beings."

"Do you need any help from me?" Li Wei asked.

"Ah! Nothing!" In turn, I asked him, "What did you want to see me about?"

"Nothing in particular. I just want to see you, Grand Master Lu. Now you're a grand Living Buddha."

We spoke for a while. I asked, "Do you still recite the Vasudhara Dharani Mantra these days?"

He replied, "Yes of course. I recited it more in the past. But now that I am busier, I recite less." His face started blushing because he was a little embarrassed.

I told him in a serious tone to never forget his mantra recitation. He nodded and replied, "Yes. Yes. Yes."

11 The Usnisa Vijaya Mantra

A man by the name of Zhao Hui came to inquire about his destiny. When he stepped into my house, I sensed that a dark cloud hovering over his head. Two ghosts were following him, but they were stopped by the door guardian outside my door. The two ghosts then started shouting.

Zhao Hui sat in front of me. I looked at him and his face appeared greyish; a stale energy lingered around him. I sighed as I observed this person from head to toe; his skin, his flesh, his bones, and all his past lives revealed nothing that was worthy of mention. What should I do?

Zhao Hui asked, "How's my destiny?"

I told him, "Seriously speaking, your destiny is something I rather not talk about."

"It's okay. Please speak frankly."

I began by saying, "Your parents died when you were young. You were raised by your relatives."

"That's right. Damn! You're good!"

"Your life was difficult during your youth. You left school and worked odd jobs, got into fights, and were sent for rehabilitation."

"That's right."

"As a teenager you became a thief and were jailed twice!"

"That's right. You even know about that!"

"Now you have achieved nothing and people avoid you."

"Yes."

"Are you still mixing with gangsters?" I asked.

Zhao Hui nodded his head. When I came to this point, I spoke no further. I knew that a person like Zhao Hui could be described with the modern term "scum bag." This was because he had never done anything decent or honorable in his life. He fooled around, led a fast life and lived loosely. He wasted away his life, and he took drugs, stole, robbed, and swindled and cheated people.

Zhao Hui asked me, "When will I become rich?"

I found this ironically amusing, but told him, "You may have to wait!"

"For how long?"

"I don't know."

Zhao Hui was not too happy and said, "People say you're the best in divination and you know everything. Now you are saying you don't know about my destiny. You better be careful."

"Sorry, but the truth is your destiny is quite challenging to predict."

"Even the most challenging life has some good fortune in it. You better tell me about my future. If I am pissed off, I'll make sure you disappear from the face of this earth!"

This was a threat! I said, "Zhao Hui, if I help you, will you do as I say?"

"Yes, I'll listen. I may be a thug, but I am not an ingrate."

I said, "I want to help you change your destiny. In actual fact, your destiny is clouded and I'm afraid you will not have any success in your life. You can become rich only by changing your destiny. If you listen to me, I can help you change your life."

"Get to the point and tell me!"

I said, "You have two ghosts following you. If these two ghosts don't leave, you'll never have a good life. Where did these two ghosts come from?"

"Two ghosts?" Zhao Hui was all confused.

"Have you killed anyone before?" I asked.

"No. I have threatened to kill, but in reality I have only hurt people, and have never killed anyone."

"Think. If you haven't killed anyone, then where did these two ghosts come from? How might you have offended ghosts before?"

Zhao Hui scratched his head and then exclaimed, "Damn! That's it! I robbed two people's graves. Is grave robbing offensive to the ghosts?"

I replied, "Of course it is."

"Damn! I only stole their burial objects. I didn't hurt anyone. What on earth are they following me for?"

"Grave robbing is a crime. If you dig up someone's grave, the dead are not going to be happy. These two ghosts are following you and you're doomed to have bad luck all the time!"

"What should I do?" Zhao Hui asked.

At that time I was thinking of teaching him a mantra which could help turn his life around. But how do I balance all the karma in his life?

- To be charitable - one receives blessings.
- To be miserly - one attracts poverty.
- To release life - one gains longevity.
- To take life - one suffers a short life.

I know that the teachings of the Buddha are supreme, extraordinary and refined. The Vajrayana mantras are like a precious mani jewel, which can fulfill all virtuous vows and accomplish all good tasks. But was Zhao Hui worthy of receiving this precious mani jewel? I reviewed the past lives of Zhao Hui and saw that in one life he was a butcher and in another he managed a brothel. In this present life, even ignoring his thefts and robberies, there was nothing good about him.

I asked Zhao Hui, "Have you done any good deeds?"

"Good deeds?" Zhao Hui shook his head.

"Do not kill, do not steal, do not commit adultery, do not lie, do not engage in worthless talk, do not gossip, do not insult, do not be greedy, do not get angry, and do not be ignorant. These are the Ten Good Deeds."

"Ha! I have committed all evils!"

"Can you think of one good thing that you have done?" I could not simply impart the precious Vajrayana teachings to someone who had committed all evil deeds.

Zhao Hui thought hard and said, "Once, I stole many things from a Buddhist temple, mainly the money donated for incense offering. I stuffed my pockets full of cash and actually carried the whole damn offering box away; they put a lock on it, but that couldn't stop me. I also took a painting off the wall and when I got home I saw that it was the picture of Shakyamuni Buddha. When I realized it was the image of the Buddha, I wanted to dump it. Damn! How much could someone get for that? I might as well have dumped it. But later, I thought it actually looked kind of nice and so I hung it on the wall. I saw that the Buddha's palms were joined together in the painting, so I joined my palms together in front of the Buddha. Is this a good deed?"

"Oh?" I was speechless.

Would you consider hanging a stolen painting of the Buddha on the wall a good deed? Was putting your palms together towards the Buddha a good deed? I was confused.

Zhao Hui said, "I did something really good. Haha!"

"What really good deed have you done?" I was surprised.

"I came to see you. That itself is a very good thing!"

"Oh!" I was again speechless.

I told Zhao Hui, "Every sentient being originally has a pure heart that is so clear, it shines like the full moon. Even if someone is a hungry ghost from the three lower realms, if he chants this mantra three times, he will receive the profound secret teachings and be liberated from the entanglement of all negative karma, and will gain all merits. If I impart this mantra to you, your destiny will change and you will have great achievement."

Zhao Hui was overjoyed and exclaimed, "Then hurry and teach me!"

I imparted the Usnisa Vijaya Dharani Mantra to Zhao Hui:

> **[transliteration:] Om, ah-mi-li-da, de-ga, fa-di, so-ha [Sanskrit: OM AMRITA TEJA VATE SVAHA].**

I took out a copy of the *Usnisa Vijaya Dharani Sutra* and showed it to Zhao Hui. The sutra says:

> **Then the Buddha told Lord Indra, "This mantra is known as the Purifying All Evil Paths Usnisa Vijaya Dharani. It can eliminate all evil karmic hindrances and eradicate the suffering of all evil paths.**
>
> **Lord of Heaven, this great dharani is proclaimed together by buddhas as numerous as eighty-eight kotis (hundred million) of the grains of sand of the Ganges River. All buddhas rejoice and uphold this dharani that is verified by the wisdom seal of the Maha Vairocana Tathagata. Lord of Heaven, if someone hears this dharani even for just a moment, he will not undergo karmic retribution from the evil karma and severe hindrances accumulated from thousands of kalpas ago, which would otherwise cause him to revolve in the cycles of birth and death - in all kinds of life forms in the evil paths - hell, hungry ghost, animal... even ants. Owing to the merits accumulated from hearing for a moment this dharani, once this very life is over, he will be reborn in the buddha pure lands, together with all the buddhas and Ekajati-pratibaddha Bodhisattvas [note: Ekajati-pratibaddha Bodhisattvas are Buddhas in**

waiting, the current one being Maitreya Bodhisattva].”

I told Zhao Hui, “Grab a handful of soil, recite this dharani twenty-one times, then scatter the soil onto the deceased, and his spirit will ascend to heaven.”

When Zhao Hui heard this, he immediately put it into action. I led Zhao Hui outside the house and instructed Zhao Hui to cast the soil in the direction as directed, and with the sound of a loud bang, the two ghosts vanished and ascended to heaven. When the two ghosts disappeared, the dark energy around Zhao Hui slowly faded away.

The Usnisa Vijaya Dharani states, “When someone recites this dharani, all his karma from a hundred kalpas will be eradicated. He will be free from serious disease and receive peace and longevity; his destiny will change and at the time of his death, he will be reborn into the various buddha pure lands.”

I imparted the Usnisa Vijaya Mudra and the visualization needed during the chanting of the mantra. One visualizes his heart transforming into a moon disc, and above this moon disc is a white Sanskrit syllable KHAM, emitting rays of light to illuminate all sentient beings. Anyone that touches this light will have his karma removed, rendering his mind and body in a state of purity. He will attain great wisdom.

* * *

Zhao Hui came up with an idea. After he had learned the Usnisa Vijaya Dharani, he practiced diligently and felt that the instruction “Grab a handful of soil, recite this dharani twenty-one times before scattering the soil onto the deceased and his spirit will ascend to heaven” was simply marvelous.

Zhao Hui told no one about this. He recited the mantra continuously with all his heart and visited a cemetery every night to scatter the mantra-empowered soil on every grave he found. It did not matter whether he knew the person in the grave or not. Zhao Hui felt that it was simply a meaningful thing to do.

When he completed scattering the soil at one public cemetery, he would proceed to another. Zhao Hui left his mark at many public graveyards.

Once, the sight of Zhao Hui frightened me: there were ghosts all over him. However, these ghosts were not here to collect debts; they were actually a community of benevolent ghosts who were here to support Zhao Hui.

I said, "You have become a ghost keeper!"

Zhao Hui replied, "This is the only way I know how to do good!"

Zhao Hui's aura had changed. The dark, greyish cloud of energy on his face had faded, replaced with a reddish and whitish glow. He appeared to be very proud of himself.

The truth was, Zhao Hui's luck had changed for the better. His health was not good before, but after chanting the mantra, he felt he had more strength. His immune system strengthened (due mainly to the support given to him by the benevolent ghosts). His illnesses healed naturally. They simply diminished without medication.

Zhao Hui had always been taking protection money from stores and street vendors in his territory. The street vendors were enjoying good business and gave him good dividends. He was not greedy and returned the dividends to the street vendors. Thus, he gained more respect.

His foster parents died and left a sum of money for him. With the money, he started a restaurant and to his surprise it made him lots of money. He invested his money and every investment was a success. He became a wealthy man.

He got married and had a son. From being the chief of the neighborhood, he rose to become a district chief, and then a magistrate of a rural township, and finally a city councilor today. Many people support Councilor Zhao. In reality, this support is caused by the many benevolent ghosts around him.

* * *

Zhao Hui told me of one incident, "The Usnisa Vijaya Mantra can protect you from physical harm!"

Zhao Hui related an incident when an opposition candidate sent a hit man to kill him. The hit man positioned himself at close range and pointed his handgun at Zhao Hui's chest. Zhao Hui immediately recited the mantra once,

> **[transliteration:] Om, ah-mi-li-da, de-ga, fa-di, so-ha**
> **[Sanskrit: OM AMRITA TEJA VATE SVAHA].**

The gunman pulled the trigger and Zhao Hui thought he was doomed. Unexpectedly, there was a cracking sound, and the bullet was stuck in the gun. The hit man shouted, "Shit! Something is spooky here!"

The hit man ran away quickly. Zhao Hui said, "This is just one example of how a crisis was averted. There are numerous cases of such miracles. In the worst of times, there will always be a turn of events to resolve any crisis. It is simply unbelievable!"

I saw the growing numbers of benevolent ghosts who had all gathered to help him, and he would likely rise from being a city councilor to a provincial councilor, and eventually a member of congress.

Here's a verse:

> **Empowering the ordinary soil with mantra**
> **This scattering of soil over the deceased is a way of the dharma**
> **When one reaches the end of the tunnel and all seems lost**
> **A new world opens and awaits him**

12 The Mantra of Light

I went to visit a small lake that was at a very secluded site. There I came across a place in the middle of a forested area which offered a spacious view of the location and also shaded me from the scorching sunlight. I set my eyes upon the glittering lake and felt relaxed and carefree.

I closed my eyes and meditated in silence. Suddenly, I heard someone whispering, "This guy is illuminating light!"

"The light is strong!"

"Will he ruin what we do here?"

"It's hard to say!"

"Let's report to Dodo!"

I opened my eyes and caught a glimpse of several kids hopping and talking under a fir tree before they disappeared in a split second. These kids were not human beings. They were little ghosts.

I stood up quietly and walked along the narrow path along the lakeside towards a nearby shop. I then asked the shop owner, "Do people often swim here?"

"Yes."

"Have any accidents happened here before?"

The shop owner did not try to avoid the subject and instead replied, "There are a few cases every year. School children love to play with water and disregard any danger. Accidents are bound to happen. The water in this lake is rather strange and there are a few areas that are quite deep actually."

"Are there any signs warning people about this lake?"

"There are," the shop owner said, "but to most school kids, it makes no difference whether there is a warning sign or not. They still swim there!"

At the lakeside, I saw several school students taking off their shirts and getting ready to enter the water. During the summer no one could resist a dip in such a fine lake.

I said nothing. After changing into my swimming trunks, I also entered the water.

The kids were splashing water towards one another, playing and pushing in their own game. Some even swam towards the deeper end of the lake. I noticed the lake appeared tranquil, but hidden beneath the surface flowed turbulent water current. The sand bed of the lake was very soft, sinking even deeper. Water weeds growing in the lake could entangle a swimmer's leg. The water closer to the shore was warmer than the water further away.

When the students were not looking, I formed a mudra with my right hand and wrote the Sanskrit syllable AH in the air and cast it in the direction of the students. I opened my divine eye.

Besides the four students swimming in the lake, I saw four little ghosts riding a wave towards the kids. But at a certain point, they were stopped by an invisible energy shield and could not proceed any further. The shield sheltered the four students, and despite many attempts, the ghosts could get no closer to the students as they had desired. In the end, the four little ghosts were exhausted and left unwillingly.

The four little ghosts darted an angry stare at me before they vanished. I returned their stare with a smirk.

The four students had fun for a while longer before they emerged from the water. I asked them, "Was it fun?"

"We had great fun. We'll come back again!"

I said, "Swimming is prohibited here. It's dangerous. The police have erected a warning notice!"

They rebutted, "Didn't you just swim in the lake yourself?"

"I…" I chuckled and could say nothing.

* * *

That night in my dream, a water ghost approached and transformed himself into a huge water snake. It was swimming in a zigzag manner around my bed, yet it could not come near me. The water ghost returned to his original form and shook his head, and out from his mouth he spat out a long strain of water weed. This water weed moved forward to wrap around my neck and tried to strangle me to death, but it stopped upon reaching my face.

The water ghost threw up gushes of water and flooded my room, attempting to drown me. Again, water filled the space around me, but not one drop of it could seep through and reach me. The water ghost vomited stinky and smelly mud and yet it could not affect me.

The water ghost realized an invisible energy field was covering the four corners of the bed, shielding me like a net of light. The bed itself was transformed into a lotus flower. I was transformed into a vajra. A net of light encircled me. The water ghost knew he had met his match and knelt down with his palms together. I asked, "Are you Dodo?"

"Yes."

"Have you harmed and taken many lives?"

"I'm ashamed of myself!"

"Why did you do it?"

Dodo replied, "So we have a chance at reincarnating to a better state."

I asked, "How did you die?"

"I committed suicide."

"Why didn't you take up spiritual cultivation?"

"I had no teacher to teach me. If I can follow you, I would achieve something." Dodo was curious and asked, "How come there is a glow around you and that you're surrounded by a net of light?"

I answered him, "This radiance and net of light is a result of my cultivation of the Mantra of Light. If you promise not to harm any more lives, I will transmit the Mantra of Light to you and you will be liberated together with your other little ghostly friends. The sutra states that if any sentient being commits the Ten Evil Deeds, the Five Deadly Sins and upon his death descends to the lower realms, reciting this mantra one hundred and eight times will allow the deceased to ascend to the Western Paradise of Ultimate Bliss. It also states that if any sentient being listens to this mantra for two, three or seven times, all his karmic hindrances will be eradicated."

The water ghost Dodo was thrilled to hear this and immediately took refuge and requested the transmission of this mantra.

I recited:

> **[transliteration:] Om, a-mo-ga, huai-lu-jia-na, ma-ha-mu-de-la, ma-ne-ba-de-ma, ji-fa-la, bo-la-fa-er-da-ya, hum [Sanskrit: OM AMOGHA VAIROCANA MAHAMUDRA MANI PADMA JVALA PRAVARTAYA HUM].**

I said, "This Mantra of Light is the Mantra of Light of the Great Empowerment of Vairocana Buddha. When you recite this mantra, visualize a moon disc in your heart, with a golden Sanskrit seed syllable AH on it. This syllable AH radiates light and illuminates on all sentient beings. Anyone in contact with this light will be liberated from suffering and receive joy. This mantra is the very Illuminated Vairocana Seal with which one may take refuge in Vairocana Tathagata. It is as good as receiving a jewel, a lotus, a rebirth and illumination, where liberation is instantaneous and all vows are fulfilled."

I told Dodo, "Tomorrow afternoon, I will write the Mantra of Light and cast it into the lake. I hope all of you will recite it diligently and be liberated."

The water ghost Dodo bowed and left.

* * *

During the afternoon on the following day, I wrote the Mantra of Light onto a piece of yellow paper and cast it into the lake. I sincerely chanted, "As the Mantra of Light enters this lake, the lake will become pure water. If commanded to wash one's feet, this water will perform this task. If commanded to wash one's knee, this water will do so. If commanded to wash one's waist, this water will carry out the work. If commanded to wash one's neck, this water will accomplish this task. If commanded to wash the internal organs, the internal organs will be purified. If commanded to clean the dirt off one's heart, the heart will become clear. If commanded to empower, one receives the Light Empowerment."

I recited:

> **As the Mantra of Light enters this lake, countless treasures lie within. The net of light spreads across the sky and all kinds of dharma sounds will be heard, spreading the words of Buddha. Surrounding the lake one will find the illumination of glowing light, dazzling in spectacular beauty. A wind of a meritorious nature blows naturally over the lake, creating ripples, offering a tenderness and warmth to the water. An intricate mix of soft and gentle fragrance also permeates the area. It is simply unimaginable.**

I saw Dodo transforming into a huge water snake, and all the little ghosts transforming into many smaller snakes. They came to the lakeside to receive the Mantra of Light Empowerment. Upon the completion of the empowerment, a wind blew across the jewel trees, creating the purest musical sound. All the water snakes received bliss and joy. The lake with its soft appearance released an all pervading fragrance. The snakes were transformed into dragons in an instant, breaking the water surface and riding on the wind towards the sky above.

13 The Eye Mara

A wealthy man in his forties by the name of Wang En once walked past a cemetery, and the wind seemed to be blowing sand into his eyes, making them red and itchy. He consulted a doctor and after some treatment his eyes were no longer red and itchy, but his vision became blurry.

Wang En's vision became poor and worsened as time passed. Though he had gone for many treatments, none had worked and eventually he became completely blind. He had to rely on a cane and the help from his family to move around.

Wang En went on like this for two years. During these two years, he consulted almost all the famous eye doctors he could find and tried out every kind of special remedy, including Chinese medicine. Whenever he heard of any person with unusual skills, he would rush over to meet him. He would also seek consultations with any famous fortune-teller and psychic medium.

Yet, his condition had not improved despite all the medication, acupuncture and special remedies. He had prayed to the gods and buddhas, but that also did not help.

That year, I returned to Taiwan from the United States to spread the dharma. Wang En sent someone to request an appointment. However, my schedule was tight and there was simply no free time left to meet any stranger. Thus, his request was turned down.

Wang En told his family, "I heard Living Buddha Sheng-yen Lu possesses great spiritual power. I must meet him!"

His family said, "He is busy."

Wang En said, "Then we will go to the airport to try our luck!"

His family said, "We heard that whenever he returns to Taiwan, thousands of people will be at the airport to welcome him. There's no way we can get near him."

Wang En exclaimed, "I must go!"

"It's useless even if you're there."

"If I go, there's a chance of meeting him. If I don't go, than there's no chance at all," Wang En insisted.

His family could not talk Wang En out of it, so they went as he wished and brought him to the international airport. If Wang En had waited for me at the arrival hall in the airport, his chances of meeting me would have been zero, as there would have been thousands of people waiting. Even my mother and mother-in-law could not get close to me. I was surrounded by the crowd and whisked away to a car that quickly drove off.

But Wang En's family had good connections in Taiwan and his friends arranged to get Wang En an entry pass, which allowed him to enter the customs and immigration checkpoints and walk straight to the arrival gate outside the door of the aircraft. This method of engagement was indeed most remarkable.

When I arrived and walked out of the docking exit, I saw a man wearing a suit and dark sunglasses, kneeling beside the aircraft door. A lady was supporting him.

The man said to me, "I am Wang En and have come specially to receive the Living Buddha."

I said, "Good! Good! Thank you!"

I helped him up. He continued to say, "I am Wang En."

I replied, "Wang En. Hmm. Wang En!" Actually I had no idea who this Wang En was!

We walked and Wang En told me, "Living Buddha! I have been sick for two years and I have become blind. I tried to meet you but was turned down, thus I have come specially to receive you, to ask you to bless my eyes so that they can see again."

When I heard this, I finally realized what it was all about. To me, these matters are a regular occurrence. Often people close in on me and ask for a blessing. But it was rare to find someone such as Wang En who actually waited and knelt at the aircraft door seeking a blessing. On his chest there was an official reception pass of the administrative personnel!

I said no more and extended my palm and pressed on Wang En's head. I also used the Sword Mudra and gently touched Wang En's eyelids.

I told him, "The blessing is done."

Wang En thanked me profusely. At this time, the group of people welcoming my arrival had approached and they also wore the official reception pass of the administrative personnel. They told me they were late because the airplane had arrived earlier than scheduled. There are many True Buddha School disciples who work in the Aviation Police Bureau, Customs, the Immigration Department and the Passport Control Bureau, etc.

When they arrived, Wang En moved even further away. I waved goodbye to Wang En but obviously he could not see that. We quickly stepped into the VIP room.

* * *

After receiving the blessing, Wang En went home. His did not regain his vision and there was hardly any improvement. Thus, it made no difference whether he had received a blessing or not.

But that very night, Wang En overheard a conversation between two voices, whispering these words.

One said, "This Living Buddha Lu almost forced the two of us out!"

The other added, "When he pressed his head once, I found myself shrinking to half my size. If he had pressed again, I would have disappeared!"

"When he touched the eyelids, it felt like an earthquake!"

"I dropped to the floor and couldn't get up!"

"Did you hurt yourself?"

"I lost much of my strength!"

"What was the scale of this earthquake?"

"I think it's at least eight on the scale!"

"Can we continue to stay here?"

"We have been here two years. I would hate to leave!"

When Wang En heard this, he was shocked! Wang En questioned these two beings, "Who are you? Are you living in my eyes? There's no hatred between us, so please leave!"

Wang En spoke, but there was no reply. He decided he should meet me one more time. After all, there was some kind of reaction, and meeting me again could help him, but his family opposed it.

"Please don't be superstitious!" His family told him.

"I really heard voices!"

"You must have imagined it!"

"This is the only time [I have heard voices]!"

His family rebutted, "This is not the first or tenth or even fiftieth time you have sought people with magical skills. Every time you went with high hopes and expectations. All of them were confident of being able to cure you, yet none of them could. In the end you always became disappointed. It's better to forget it!"

Wang En pleaded, "Just this once. I really heard voices!"

"It's probably a dream!"

"Only this once, please!" Wang En kept pleading.

* * *

During my Taiwan dharma tour, my schedule had been very tight. Grand dharma ceremonies were conducted in northern, central and southern Taiwan, at stadiums that were packed to full capacity. Besides, I had to visit every local chapter and dharma center in Taiwan.

Once, while eating at a restaurant, an attendant said to another, "Should we report to Grand Master?"

"I think we better not. Grand Master is too busy!"

I turned around and asked, "What's the matter?"

The attendant replied, "A blind man named Wang En has been following us for two or three days in a car, and he kept requesting a meeting with Grand Master. We have turned him down many times, but he won't give up. We almost can't take it anymore!"

"Ah! Wang En! I know him! Please let him in!"

Wang En and his family were quickly led into the restaurant. I gave Wang En another blessing. I said, "I have this *Clear Vision Sutra* and Clear Vision Mantra. I am passing this to your family, so that they can teach you how to recite them. The eyes will radiate light when you recite the sutra, thus clearing all darkness."

Wang En was overjoyed. I wrote *The Clear Vision Sutra* and handed it to Wang En's family.

The Clear Vision Sutra as Spoken by the Buddha:

Namo the All Illuminating Ksitigarbha Bodhisattva [three times]. The Thousand-arms Thousand-eyes Avalokitesvara Bodhisattva. The two eyes resemble two golden lamps. In the west, where the Buddha throne is, lies a pagoda. In the assembly of the Tathagata exists one sutra. Manjushri Bodhisattva is riding his lion. Samantabhadra Bodhisattva is riding on the elephant king. The two eyes resemble heaven. Mara within man. Mara within the eyes. All the hindrances within the eyes will be removed. Veil within man.

Veil within the eyes. All the clouds and fog within the eyes will be cleared. Clarity within man. Clarity within the eyes. All the light spots within the eyes are glowing brightly. Whoever recites this *Clear Vision Sutra* will gain clear vision in every life. Mahamayuri Vidyarajni is spiritually in tune. Avalokitesvara Bodhisattva offers peace and tranquility. [transliteration:] Om, xi-dian-duo, bo-ju-na [Sanskrit: OM SIDDAMTA BAJUNA]. Namo the All Illuminating Ksitigarbha Bodhisattva Soha.

I handed *The Clear Vision Sutra* to Wang En's family. Wang En was very happy to receive *The Clear Vision Sutra* and regarded it as a jewel. This sutra only records the names of bodhisattvas and a small line of mantra. This makes it very easy to memorize. Before long, Wang En was able to recite the sutra by heart.

Wang En recited the sutra countless times every day. On the forty-ninth day, during the afternoon, a roll of thunder sounded in the sky. Wang En was frightened by it and was shivering, and then he felt two objects roll out of his eyes. These things seemed like tears but they were not tears, and they were like beads but they were not. Once they rolled out, everything changed. In fact when the thunder and lightning came, Wang En not only heard the thunder, but also sensed the lightning flashes as well.

His eyesight improved every day since that day. Little by little he could see things again and eventually, he fully regained his vision. Wang En exclaimed, "Hooray to Grand Master Lu! Hooray for *The Clear Vision Sutra*! My eyes have finally recovered!"

This is:

While it is true that all things are subject to nature's law
Recovery from illnesses depends upon good affinity
When one obtains a genuine sutra one will become as clear as the mirror

Within this clarity everything in the world will be reflected

* * *

One time during my tour to spread the dharma, I was sitting on the dharma throne when I felt something fly into my eyes, causing irritation and prickling. My eyes became red and I felt very uncomfortable.

That night, I went to bed after applying some eye drops. I also heard some voices, "Grand Master Lu, Living Buddha Lu, pardon our intrusion."

Confused, I questioned, "What's the matter?"

"We were the tenants of Wang En but he has just chased us out. Since you forced us out of him, we are moving into your house!"

I instantly knew what was going on.

"Are you the maras within the eye?"

"That's right."

"What will happen to my eyes?"

"Blindness," the eye maras said.

"I can drive you away from Wang En. What makes you think I can't get rid of you the same way?"

The eye maras said, "You're too involved in the game to see things objectively."

I asked them, "How many people have you victimized?"

"Countless."

I said, "Very well then! You have harmed many people and now you have come looking for trouble with the wrong person. I won't let you off the hook!"

The eye maras shouted, "We're not afraid of you!"

I shut my eyes tightly to seal off their escape. Water poured out from within my eyes and this water was not ordinary water. It was the "mythical low-buoyancy water" that flows below Kunlun Mountain. Not even a feather can float on it. Water flowed in continuously, turning my eyes into two great oceans. The two eye maras yelled, "We're drowning. We can't swim. Let us out of here!"

I said, "No way!"

Eventually, the two eye maras drowned. These evil beings who had caused so much harm to others finally had a taste of their own medicine.

I, Living Buddha Sheng-yen Lu, suffered no harm at all!

14 The Boomerang Shield Mantra

The basis of Vajrayana teachings depends on three factors of cultivation. These three factors are:

- Mantra (dharani)
- Mudra (hand mudra, body mudra)
- Visualization (power of concentration)

This means using your mouth to chant mantras, using your hands to form mudras, and using your mind to visualize the personal deity [Tibetan: yidam] in your practice. Thus, our "body, speech and mind" become purified, achieving the goal of transforming "the Three Karmas into the Three Secrets." This kind of cultivation method constitutes the practice of Vajrayana.

Padmasambhava, the founder of the Nyingma School of Tibetan Buddhism, once faced the attack of five hundred heretics during his journey of cultivation. These five hundred heretics chanted spells to invoke the descent of evil spirits and vicious gods and attempted to take Padmasambhava's life with the use of magical power.

Padmasambhava found himself in an extremely critical situation and was pushed to the verge of death. These five hundred heretics were all high priests of their respective cults who had practiced their art for many years. They could summon the wind and rain at will and cast out beans that turned into soldiers. They were also adepts at summoning spirits.

Padmasambhava collapsed upon reaching a huge tree and his life was hanging by a thread! At that moment, Simhamukha appeared. [Simhamukha is also known as the Lion-Faced Dakini.] She is the guru, the personal deity as well as the dharma protector of Padmasambhava, all rolled in one.

Simhamukha imparted the Boomerang Shield Mantra to Padmasambhava. This mantra is of the highest secret among all secrets, and would not be transmitted to anyone who is not qualified.

It would not be transmitted to the following types of people:

1. A malevolent person.
2. A person not within the lineage.
3. A person who has a fickle heart.
4. A person who cannot keep secrets.

What constitutes a person whose heart is fickle? Most students who follow a master would display their loyalty and obedience. Yet, as the days and months pass, they would have a change of heart. Examples of these disciples include the likes of Devadatta, Judas and countless others.

This Boomerang Shield Mantra is a supreme mantra, and holds great importance. Thus it should not be imparted indiscriminately.

What exactly is the Boomerang Shield Mantra?

1. The Boomerang Effect - whatever spell that is cast would be returned back to the spell-caster, and he would receive the full effect of the spell.

2. The Shield Effect - whatever spell that is cast would be blocked, rendering the spell completely useless against the person it was cast.

When Padmasambhava received the Boomerang Shield Mantra from Simhamukha, he recited the mantra and retaliated. A clap of thunder sounded and the fog dispersed, revealing the stiff bodies of the five hundred heretics who had been killed by the shock wave of the Boomerang Shield Mantra. This is the famous Boomerang Shield Mantra psychic battle.

* * *

A female disciple of mine had a friend named Feng Fang. This Feng Fang was such an enchanting beauty that someone once described her through a love letter this way:

"You carry yourself with the grace and elegance of a swan. Your every step ripples like the blossoming white lotus flower upon the shimmering green water. Your slim waistline firms up as though a silk scarf is wrapped around it. Your slender neckline, your arms, your ankles, and your face of such fair complexion certainly need no makeup. Your beauty is unmatched by anyone. Your silky dark hair flows like the waterfall and your eyebrows curve like the silver moon. Your cherry-like, sweet-scented red lips shield a row of white teeth that line up like tiny seashells. Your clear bright eyes glisten with such charm..."

Feng Fang's beauty was praised by all. Most importantly, Feng Fang carried herself with ease and confidence, and glowed with a natural charismatic aura. She had many admirers.

One of them was an evil sorcerer, who had a notorious reputation. He too wrote love letters to Feng Fang:

> Your beauty is unsurpassed throughout all time.
> As a gesture of my admiration,
> I offer you precious gems handed down from my ancestors.

I ask God to be my matchmaker.
Please do not reject me.
Do not be heartless.
Now that I have you,
My search is finally over.

This evil sorcerer was really good at writing poetry! Unfortunately for him, Feng Fang did not like him, and thus rejected him. The evil sorcerer was furious and he told people, "There's nothing extraordinary about Feng Fang. Women like her are a dime a dozen. Since she thinks nothing of me, I will show her my power. I want her to suffer for the rest of her life and come begging for my mercy. Even if she comes and begs, I would ignore her."

The evil sorcerer told this to not just one person, but many others. Feng Fang was not afraid and did not take it seriously. However, the evil sorcerer conducted a ritual and cast a spell on her. He used the blood of a white chicken to draw a talisman and jade to empower the talisman. He also offered high quality rice to the spirits...

The spiritual entity that the evil sorcerer enshrined was unusual. Its body was black and it had two heads. It had ferocious features and it held two snakes, a green one on the left and red one on the right. This deity was known as the "Mental Disorder Ghost."

One night, Feng Fang saw the evil sorcerer in her dream and he was conducting a ritual on her. Her head was completely pierced with needles dipped in chicken blood.

When she woke up, she was delirious. Subsequently, she suffered from insomnia and could not sleep at night, despite all attempts to fall asleep. She went on pills and initially she could sleep, but eventually the medication could not help her. She had become despondent and miserable, and her face was drained of its bright appearance. In the end, she suffered a mental collapse and went mad.

The psychiatrist diagnosed her as suffering from delusion of persecution. Feng Fang felt that a large organization was out to harm her.

Examples were such that when a plane was flying over the sky, she would imagine the plane was there to spy on her. When the mailman delivered mail, she would think that he was a crook disguised as a mailman to assassinate her.

Feng Fang's cats and dogs were given away because she felt their spirits had been seized by evil people and replaced with the spirits of malevolent people who wanted to harm her.

Food cooked for her was considered poisoned, unless she had cooked it herself.

She bathed many times every day as she felt that she was touched by something filthy and that no amount of washing can clean away all of the filth. She had to wash her own clothes over and over again every day. Everyone she saw had been polluted and stained, and she was afraid of contamination.

She also uttered nonsense, laughed out loud, and giggled secretly by herself. Sometimes she cried because she had felt that there were no good people in the world and everyone was out to harm her! She would not sleep and eat. Yet occasionally she would sleep for two to three consecutive days, and at times she would not sleep at all, screaming and shouting. If she thought of something, she would go and do it.

Her condition had deteriorated to the point where she would undress and run to the marketplace. She would dump food in the middle of a road, and she would break all light bulbs, claiming that all objects that gave off light were of the devil.

This is similar to an ancient poem:

Self is clearly the object
On which misfortune could attach and befall
You must know that illness spares nobody
Just as one thinks of stopping idle thoughts
The very thought itself is but a delusion
Even if you find what you hold as true reality

The reality itself may hold little truth
All illnesses are the result of karma
Clearing one's karma is the best solution
Thus self-cultivation will lead one out of life and death
And all disaster will then turn to dust

Feng Fang was once a really beautiful woman, but as her illness lingered, her body became repulsive and resembled that of a skeleton. Feng Fang was led to seek my help by my disciple. I wrote a "Shang Yan" Talisman to help shield her, but it did not work! I set up a spiritual boundary around her, but it was also ineffective!

I was worried. I decided to sit in meditation and observe the situation. When half of an incense stick that I lit had burned away, I suddenly had a vision of a forest with a path that led to an altar. I saw a man dressed in black, praying to a rather bizarre looking deity. This was the same completely dark spirit that I mentioned earlier. I saw the man in black armed with a blood-stained knife butchering a lady. This lady was none other than Feng Fang herself!

I was shocked to see this. I asked the family of Feng Fang about this matter and her family confirmed it. Her family told me that Feng Fang had rejected the sorcerer and thus offended the man. The sorcerer had indeed cast a spell on Feng Fang and some people witnessed it. The sorcerer himself had told many others that he wanted Feng Fang to suffer for the rest of her life!

Normally, applying the Shang Yan Talisman and setting a spiritual boundary are very powerful and effective, yet this sorcerer and the deity were even more powerful. This came as a shock to me.

Later, I searched the ancient books and found a reference to the deity. It was not actually called the Mental Disorder Ghost but instead was an ancient spirit that had lived for thousands of years; it is known as Qiang. As this spirit was ancient, the Shang Yan Talisman and spiritual boundary had no effect against it.

I felt I should talk with this sorcerer. I believed that a face-to-face meeting would at least set some ground for discussion. If the other party was reasonable in any way, it should not be a problem to work things out.

I finally met up with the sorcerer. His family name was Gu and his sorcery skills were taught to him by a master from Mainland China. His disciples feared him, as his mastery of spell casting was extremely powerful. Anyone who had been a victim of his spell would have suffered insanity.

I said, "I came here because of Feng Fang!"

Sorcerer Gu replied, "She doesn't appreciate me! She deserves what she got!"

"Can you let her off? She has suffered enough, and she should have learned her lesson by now." I was trying to appeal to his humanity.

Sorcerer Gu said, "Everyone knows I have cast a spell on Feng Fang. My business has prospered because of her insanity. Who are you to demand that I release her?"

"I am Sheng-yen Lu!"

"So I see. You do enjoy a small reputation. Wouldn't it be interesting if you were to suffer from my spell?"

"Look! We have no scores to settle with each other. I am here to appeal for her release!"

"You're appealing to me? It sounds more like you're picking a fight! What if I don't let Feng Fang off? Do you want to challenge me to a psychic battle?"

"No!"

"Go home Sheng-yen Lu. Let's see who's better!"

"No!" I said.

Sorcerer Gu simply ignored me and attended to his own business. I felt I had just bumped into a wall, getting absolutely nowhere with the conversation; so much for an appeal to his humanity.

The matter did not end here however. This sorcerer Gu had invoked the presence of Qiang to cast a spell on me. My fence of protection had been completely neutralized. This meant that my dharma protectors had abandoned me when they realized they were no match for Qiang; even the umbrella shield that I set up during my sleeping hours was gone.

I felt dizzy and I became extremely hot-tempered. I would feel cold for a while, and then feel hot, and my mind was a blank. I had no appetite for food and everything had no taste.

I could not sleep well, and when I fell asleep, I kept having strange and chaotic dreams. I felt as though my body was burning in flames.

I felt that life had lost its meaning to me and I found no reason to live. The thought of wanting to die grew ever stronger. Indeed, once a person dies everything dies with him. No matter how hard one tries, either to be a hero, or a saintly practitioner, or to acquire fame and fortune, eventually we all end up dead.

Maybe I should die! This life is one of pain and sorrow, filled with only emptiness and impermanence. I felt that life was meaningless.

Then, it dawned upon me that I had fallen under the sorcerer's spell!

I found that the joints all over my body were in pain and it seemed that all kinds of illnesses were about to break out. I could not enter into meditation and even if I managed to do so, I had visions of green and red snakes crawling all over and within me.

This Qiang was indeed a powerful ancient deity. I could not think of any method to counter it. I began to hallucinate, seeing and hearing things. I felt I was on the verge of a mental breakdown.

At that time it was simply:

Finding the mountains misty and the waters chilly
Everything appears empty as I go crazy
I see a tiger growling beneath the cliff
Then see a clay figurine running among the trees

As the wind blows and the solar heat dissipates
Illusory, rain-soaked flowers gradually fall away
There is no place on earth I can truly stay
Should any immortal suffer from this
He would have snapped and gone mad anyway

I saw a green snake and a red snake sliding into my urinary system, resulting in an unusual illness which forced me to run to the bathroom every five minutes. Yet, each time it was nothing more than just a few drops of urine, but the urgency caused by the need to urinate was overpowering; this was excessive urination.

There were times when I felt my bladder was full and needed to use the bathroom. But when I reached the toilet, I could not urinate at all. I considered seeking help from doctors who could treat my urination problem.

When I could urinate, I would feel the immediate need to urinate again. Besides urination, my bowel movements were equally tormenting. I felt nauseated and dizzy, losing my sense of balance. No doctor visits or doctor-prescribed medicine could cure me of my illness, and I felt that this period of eating and sleeping disorders was a living hell.

Fierce deities and demons appeared before me, entered my body, resulting in inflammation and malfunction in all of my internal organs. I pondered over the subject of death.

I felt that the suffering of illness would rank as the worst of all sufferings in the world. I felt that once someone's body and mind suffer from any chronic disease or terminal illness, it would be better for him to die. Seriously speaking, if there would have been some kind of happy and peaceful way to die, I would have been very willing to embrace it.

I thought of committing suicide. Many people with long-term illnesses cannot take the pain of the suffering and after struggling to leave their beds, they commit suicide. I used to think that these patients who took their own lives were foolish, but I had gained a new perspective. Only those who have experienced the tormenting agony of a serious illness would understand why these patients have chosen to kill themselves. The ordeal of suffering from a serious illness is definitely the greatest suffering in the world.

I saw no value in being alive, as I had saved many lives and was persecuted just as many times. Having reached this point, I felt no reason to go on living.

I was wrestling with myself at the edge of life and death!

As the sun is bound to set in the west
The spirit awaiting judgment lingers in the spiritual world
Enlightenment is certainly within oneself
One must decide if he will be filial

Think about it: Living Buddha Lian-sheng, Sheng-yen Lu had committed suicide! The Lotus Light Unhindered Buddha had killed himself! Padmakumara had taken his own life!

This was against my earlier stand that committing suicide meant killing a buddha. The physical body is the means to attaining buddhahood, and thus committing suicide is the same as killing a buddha.

Those who have committed suicide cannot enter heaven, and will reincarnate in the three lower realms. They suffer from a lack of wisdom and, even if they are reborn as human beings, they will be born with disabilities.

I am a spiritual guide to many, and if I were to kill myself, it would certainly be a big joke! However, all of the eight kinds of suffering that Shakyamuni Buddha had mentioned converged on me. My suffering was indescribable! I could not bear it anymore! I really did not want to live anymore!

If I had committed suicide, it would become a subject of ridicule. The founder of True Buddha School, Living Buddha Lian-sheng,

Sheng-yen Lu, had committed suicide! Would True Buddha School continue to exist?

It would be agonizing to those who were close to me, and exhilarating to those who hated me. What a diversity of emotion it would be!

When sorcerer Gu spiritually beheaded me with his magical power, the green and red snakes slipped into my head. My head then split into eight petals! In the middle appeared a shrine and my personal deity, Amitabha Buddha, was seated in stillness. You might say that I was dead and only this personal deity remained. This is the very essence of my years of cultivation.

Sorcerer Gu wanted to destroy my personal deity. The green and red snakes wanted to devour my personal deity. Unperturbed by this, Amitabha Buddha recited the Boomerang Shield Mantra once, "..............."

A stroke of lightning flashed:

When one's arms and limbs are separated
What is left of this bodily form
Besides losing one's features and image
One's name and identity is void and gone

Just as the autumn grass paints the tide of life
The twilight wind speaks the truth of one's changing figure
I ask that you discern from a higher perspective
And contemplate more on this matter

Never push someone into a corner
Never push me into a corner

My personal deity Amitabha Buddha recited the Boomerang Shield Mantra once and there appeared a flash of lightning. I found myself lying on the bed motionless; my body was completely exhausted like someone who was half dead. Yet, I was aware that the green and red snakes had vanished, and so had sorcerer Gu.

In the space above, I saw the green and red snakes biting sorcerer Gu, refusing to let go. His struggle to break free only made the snakes tighten around him even more.

Sorcerer Gu's sad and shrill cries streaked across the night sky!

All symptoms of my illness suddenly disappeared, and my health improved, and I recovered completely after a week. In Feng Fang's case, her symptoms also vanished suddenly, and she snapped out of her mental daze. After a period of rest and rehabilitation, her health returned to normal.

To me, it seemed like a nightmare, and to Feng Fang, the nightmare had stretched even longer! In sorcerer Gu's case, he was attacked by the same ancient evil deity, Qiang, whom he had prayed to, and he could not escape. In the end, he became mad!

* * *

I just want to let you know how important this Boomerang Shield Mantra is. It is supreme, all important, and must be shielded in secrecy. Thus, I can only impart this mantra in secret and cannot share it here.

This incident taught me a great lesson. I must focus on the importance of reciting mantras, keep a pure and unattached state of mind, and take my cultivation seriously.

This is:

The primal state of Vajrayana
Is anchored in mantra
You should keep your mind pure
And dignify the body

Untouched by all

And focus on helping others
Remove your karma
And increase your wisdom

Unite with your personal deity
And attain the highest purity
Devote actively to liberating sentient beings
Yet maintain a simple lifestyle

Forge ahead with your cultivation vigorously
While holding proper thoughts and being respectful
Month after month and year after year
Without beginning, without ending

Om Ah Hum

Students are protected by thirty-six guardians after taking refuge, which are sent by the Four Heavenly Kings (devarajas). If these students can also cultivate the Root Guru Practice, then Vajrayaksa, his retinue of five hundred, and multitudes of bodhisattvas will also provide protection.

The Sutra of Consecration

The True Buddha Sutra

The Sutra of Authentic Dharma that Removes Hindrances and Bestows Good Fortune

(This *True Buddha Sutra* is the spontaneous revelation from the heart of Living Buddha Lian-sheng, the emanation body of White Mahapadmakumara of the Maha Twin Lotus Ponds in the Western Paradise.)

Supplication for the blessing of Living Buddha Lian-sheng:

OM, AH, HUM.

With reverence I make my purified body, speech, and mind an offering to Vairocana. The holy Buddhalocana is the dharma body, Padmakumara is the bliss body, and Living Buddha Lian-sheng is the emanation body; these three bodies being the same in essence as the Buddha's grace.

Homage to his True Buddha lineage and his transcendent power that encompasses the whole universe. Radiating light throughout the Three Times, he can manifest himself instantaneously. Disciples of Buddha should constantly cry out for his pure light which enhances blessings and wisdom.

In the past, his buddhahood was prophesied by Shakyamuni Buddha and he was entrusted with the mission of salvation by Amitabha Buddha. Maitreya Bodhisattva bestowed upon him the Red Crown and Guru Padmasambhava taught him the Tantra.

We pray you never abandon your vows to liberate us all. Thus, as you embrace and enfold us with protection and care, empower us to quickly attain realization.

Namo Vairocana Buddha.
Namo Buddhalocana.
Namo Padmakumara.
Namo Living Buddha Lian-sheng.

Namo the True Buddha Assembly, all buddhas, bodhisattvas, and mahasattvas everywhere throughout the Three Times (3 times).

Recite the Sacred Edict three times:

The Western True Buddha Assembly, the Maha Twin Lotus Ponds, the Eighteen Mahapadmakumaras, the Holy Revered One Robed in White, the Holy Red Crown Vajra Master, the Lord of Secrets of the Realm of Vajra-mantra, the Great Enlightened Founder of Ling Xian True Buddha School: the Eminent Tantric Adept Sheng-yen Lu.

Incense Praise:

The incense is now lit, suffusing the dharma realm, and from afar the scent is inhaled by the True Buddha Assembly. Auspicious are the gathering clouds, as we now request, with sincere and earnest hearts, that all buddhas manifest.
Namo cloud canopy of fragrance, bodhisattvas, mahasattvas.
Namo cloud canopy of fragrance, bodhisattvas, mahasattvas.
Namo cloud canopy of fragrance, bodhisattvas, mahasattvas.

Namo True Buddha Assembly, all buddhas, bodhisattvas and mahasattvas. (three times)

Invocation of the Two Buddhas and Eight Bodhisattvas:

Namo Vairocana Buddha of the All-Conquering Palace in the Dharma Realm.
Namo Amitabha Buddha of the Western Paradise.
Namo Mahasattva Avalokitesvara.
Namo Mahasattva Maitreya.
Namo Mahasattva Akasagarbha.
Namo Mahasattva Samantabhadra.
Namo Mahasattva Vajrapani.
Namo Mahasattva Manjusri.
Namo Mahasattva Nivaranaviskambin.
Namo Mahasattva Ksitigarbha.
Namo all bodhisattvas and mahasattvas.

Sutra Opening Verse:

The most supreme profound dharma,
Is rarely encountered in hundreds and thousands of kalpas,
As I receive this transmission and blessing,
I vow to penetrate the true meaning of the Tathagata.

The Sutra of Authentic Dharma that Removes Hindrances and Bestows Good Fortune, spoken by Living Buddha Lian-sheng:

Thus, have I heard. At one time, White Mahapadmakumara was present at the Maha Twin Lotus Ponds, sitting upon the great white lotus dharma throne; surrounding him were seventeen other great lotus blossoms. The Green Lotus radiated green light, the Yellow Lotus yellow light, the Red Lotus red light, the Purple Lotus purple light. Each lotus blossom was mysteriously wonderful, pure, and full of fragrance.

White Padmakumara, silently calling forth his spiritual power, transformed the Maha Twin Lotus Ponds into an extraordinarily splendid place filled with golden light. All the flower buds simultaneously burst into fragrant blossoms. Jade grasses sent forth a wonderful scent. White cranes, peacocks, parrots, saris, kalavinkas, and jivajivas all took on a golden hue, and sang graceful heavenly songs in harmony.

The sky filled with golden light. A pure and wonderful heavenly melody resounded from the sky. Fragrances suffused all realms. Golden sky-abodes, adorned throughout with golden lotuses, radiated splendor. From the sky there showered heavenly flowers.

At that moment, the ground shook violently in the Maha Twin Lotus Ponds and throughout countless heavens tremors could be felt. Buddhas, bodhisattvas, and sound-hearers all felt it as well and came to the Maha Twin Lotus Ponds, as did the rulers of all the Thirty-three Heavens. The assembly included beings from the Twenty-eight Heavens, Lords Indra and Brahma, the eight classes of supernatural beings, and the fourfold assembly, all of whom came to hear the revelation of quintessential teaching.

At that moment, the Golden Padmakumara emitted the Great Wisdom Light. The White Padmakumara emitted the Dharma Realm Light. The Green Padmakumara emitted the Ten Thousand Treasure Light. The Black Padmakumara emitted the Subjugation Light. The Red Padmakumara emitted the Vow Light. The Purple Padmakumara emitted the Majestic Light. The Blue Padmakumara emitted the Virtuous Fruition Light. The Yellow Padmakumara emitted the Fortune Fulfilling Light. The Orange Padmakumara emitted the Child Innocence Light.

Upon seeing this, all the heavenly beings were greatly awed. Then Indra arose from his seat and, joining his palms to White Padmakumara, said, "This is most rare, O Holy and Revered One. By what cause does the Maha Twin Lotus Ponds emit such great light and splendor?"

White Mahapadmakumara said, "I will expound upon this for everyone present." Indra said, "The Holy Revered One is the most mighty and powerful. Please explain to everyone present, that all men and devas may know where to turn."

At that moment, White Mahapadmakumara addressed Indra and the assembly as follows: "Very well, very well. I will now explain to you and all the beings of the last period of this Buddha-kalpa, and all those in the future who have an affinity with the sutra, so that all may know the True Buddha Tantra and the principle that removes hindrances and bestows good fortune."

White Mahapadmakumara then said, "All buddhas and bodhisattvas have, in order to liberate living beings, manifested the worlds known as 'All-Conquering,' 'Wonderful Treasure,' 'Round Pearl,' 'Sorrowless,' 'Pure Rest,' 'Dharma Thought,' 'Full Moon,' 'Profound Joy,' 'Profound Completeness,' 'Lotus,' 'Immutable,' and 'Omnipresence.' Now, there shall be the 'True Buddha World.'"

Thus, the buddhas, bodhisattvas, sound-hearers, solitary-buddhas, and all the heavenly beings witnessed the Holy Revered One bringing forth the True Buddha World, understanding it to be a manifestation of the cause and fruition of great compassion of the auspicious well-departed ones of the past, present, and future, and realizing that the Holy Revered One came for the sake of all beings. All present were moved by joy as never before. Then, bowing their heads, they made praise with these verses:

The Holy Revered One of great compassion,
The Secret One who is most supreme,
Had attained enlightenment in the past,
And transcended all worldly passions.
He now establishes the True Buddha World,
Showering compassion on all living beings.
Transforming himself into a pure land founding buddha,

He descends into the saha world.
With Lian-sheng as his name,
He announces and proclaims the dharma to all.
We all now have heard,
And shall vow to protect and uphold his dharma.

At that moment, the holy revered White Mahapadmakumara instructed the assembly, saying "In cultivation, the key to realizing the Buddha Jewel Sambodhi is a quiescent mind; that of realizing the Dharma Jewel is purity of body, speech, and mind; that of realizing the Sangha Jewel is refuge in a True Buddha Guru."

The Holy Revered One further instructed the assembly, saying "If good men or women, on the eighteenth day of the fifth month of each lunar year, make ablution, abstain from meat, and wear new and clean clothes, or on the eighteenth day of each lunar month, or on their own birthdays, call upon the Two Buddhas and Eight Bodhisattvas before the shrine, and reverently recite this *Sutra of Authentic Dharma that Removes Hindrances and Bestows Good Fortune*, then their supplications will be answered. Moreover, if incense, flowers, lamps, tea and fruit are offered, along with sincere prayer, then all wishes will be granted."

The Holy Revered One told the assembly, "People of this saha world, be they high officials, nobility, renunciates, householders, yogis, or common folk, who, upon learning of this sutra, uphold, recite, print and propagate it, shall prosper above all others, have greater lifespan, obtain either a son or daughter as sought, and be blessed with measureless fortune. This is indeed a great fortune-bestowing sutra for obtaining blessings.

One may have ancestors, enemies, close ones or creditors who are unable to obtain liberation and remain lost in the nether world. However, by upholding, reciting, printing, and propagating this sutra, the deceased will ascend to heaven, enemies will be turned away, and those living will be blessed. If there be a man or woman seized by negative forces or afflicted by spirits, or confused and haunted by nightmares, then, by upholding, reciting, printing, and propagating this sutra, all negative influences shall be banished, thereby restoring peace and ease.

If one suffers the physical retribution of illness and calamity, whether due to non-virtuous body karma from previous lives or to the afflictions of spirits, then, by upholding, reciting, printing and propagating this sutra, ill omens will immediately disappear and the causes of illness will quickly be removed. If one suffers from misfortune, legal entanglements or imprisonment, then, by upholding, reciting, printing and propagating this sutra, all such obstacles will dissolve immediately, and calamities will be vanquished and turned into auspiciousness.

Should nations enter into war, then whoever upholds this sutra and enthrones the image of Padmakumara, setting up offerings before it, immediately receives extra prowess wherein no battle can be lost. Those who uphold, recite, print, or propagate this sutra will receive all blessings, just as they desire. All hindrances will be removed, and the sufferings of the cycle of birth and death will be extinguished."

Then, in the Western True Buddha Assembly at the Maha Twin Lotus Ponds, White Mahapadmakumara proclaimed this mantra:

"Om, gu-ru, lian-sheng sid-dhi, hum."

When the Holy Revered One completed this discourse, Indra and the whole assembly, including devas, nagas, the rest of the eight classes of supernatural beings, and the fourfold assembly, all paid reverence. They brought forth faith and upheld the teaching.

Thus ends *The Sutra of Authentic Dharma that Removes Hindrances and Bestows Good Fortune.*

Thus, the buddhas, bodhisattvas, sound-hearers, solitary-buddhas, and all the heavenly beings witnessed the Holy Revered One bringing forth the True Buddha World, understanding it to be a manifestation of the cause and fruition of great compassion of the auspicious well-departed ones of the past, present, and future, and realizing that the Holy Revered One came for the sake of all beings. All present were moved by joy as never before.

The True Buddha Sutra

Significance of Taking Refuge

Taking refuge means to accept guidance, reliance and deliverance.

The heart of taking refuge lies in one word: faith. Faith is the beginning of all endeavors, just as the saying goes:

> **Faith is the basis of the path, the mother of virtues;**
> **Nourishing and growing all good ways,**
> **Cutting away the net of doubts,**
> **Revealing the unsurpassed road to enlightenment.**

The doctrine of faith, understanding, practice, and realization as taught in Buddhism begins with faith.

Taking refuge and receiving the respective empowerments are similar to a student officially registering for enrollment in school. When one receives the empowerment from Living Buddha Lian-sheng and takes refuge in him, one also receives the lineage transmission of True Buddha School and formally becomes a disciple of the school. One's negative karma gradually dissolves, and one is protected by the thirty-six benevolent deities. One also receives all kinds of merits, and does not easily fall into the Three Evil Paths. Therefore, one is able to swiftly accumulate good karma, and eventually realize supreme enlightenment.

From the discussion above, one can thus see that the ritual of taking refuge and empowerment is a holy and noble undertaking. Once one receives the refuge empowerment, one truly enters the gate of practicing Buddhism and becomes a True Buddha disciple.

However, taking refuge is not the same as ordination (becoming a monk or nun). Any ordination must have the written and signed consent from one's parents or spouse, and it must be officially approved by the highest authority of True Buddha School.

The Sutrayana tradition practices the Threefold Refuge, whereas the Vajrayana tradition practices the Fourfold Refuge.

In the Fourfold Refuge, the meaning of the Sanskrit word "Namo" is to take refuge.

Namo Guru bei – I take refuge in the Root Guru.
Namo Buddha ye – I take refuge in the Buddha.
Namo Dharma ye – I take refuge in the Dharma.
Namo Sangha ye – I take refuge in the Sangha or the ordained.

Significance of Taking Refuge in Living Buddha Lian-Sheng and True Buddha School

The Merits of Taking Refuge

Living Buddha Lian-sheng has the dharma title of "Great Blessing Vajra" and he is the Root Guru of True Buddha School. True Buddha disciples who cultivate the Root Guru Practice will be able to achieve spiritual union and responses from the Root Guru, which is a great blessing. With the Root Guru's blessing, one can gain health, long life, a harmonious family, fortune, wisdom, and the fulfillment of all wishes in the mundane realm. In the transcendental realm, one attains bodhisattvahood.

According to *The Sutra of Consecration,* students are protected by thirty-six guardians after taking refuge, which are sent by the Four Heavenly Kings (devarajas). If these students can also cultivate the Root Guru Practice, then Vajrayaksa, his retinue of five hundred, and multitudes of bodhisattvas will also provide protection.

All students who take refuge and receive the necessary empowerments shall, through the diligent cultivation of the Root Guru Practice, benefit both themselves and others due to the boundless merits of the Root Guru Practice. All transgressions will be extinguished and all evil shall depart. The Root Guru Practice is the most efficacious of all practices and should be widely propagated.

The Methods of Taking Refuge

At 7:00 a.m. (your local time), on either the first or the fifteenth of every lunar month, face the direction of the rising sun. With palms joined, reverently recite the Fourfold Refuge Mantra three times: "Namo Guru bei, Namo Buddha ye, Namo Dharma ye, Namo Sangha ye. Seeking Living Buddha Lian-sheng's guidance, I am taking refuge in the True Buddha," and prostrate three times.

Send a letter to the True Buddha Foundation to indicate your wish to receive the refuge empowerment. State your name, address, age, and enclose a voluntary offering to the contact address of Living Buddha Lian-sheng. Upon receiving the letter, the True Buddha Foundation will process your request. The address is:

Grand Master Sheng-yen Lu
17102 NE 40th Ct.
Redmond, WA 98052
U.S.A.
Tel: 425-885-7573
Fax: 425-883-2173

Upon receiving the refuge request letter, the True Buddha Foundation will send you a refuge certificate, a picture of Living Buddha Lian-sheng, and instructions on how to start cultivation of the Four Preliminary Practices.

You may obtain refuge empowerment personally from Grand Master Lu, or from a True Buddha acharya who confers the empowerment on behalf of Grand Master, by visiting a True Buddha temple, chapter, cultivation group, or by attending a True Buddha ceremony.

Glossary

Amitabha (Sanskrit, literally "Boundless Light")
One of the Five Dhyani Buddhas. Typically depicted with a red body and holding the Meditation Mudra.

Ananda
One of principal disciples, a devout attendant, and a cousin of Shakyamuni Buddha. Amongst the Buddha's many disciples, Ananda had the most retentive memory and many sutras are attributed to his recollection of the Buddha's teachings during the First Buddhist Council.

Attached Spirit
Spiritual entities who follow or attach themselves to the body of an individual and oftentimes cause disturbances (illness, accidents, misfortune, etc.).

Bardo Deliverance
This practice is to assist spirits who are between rebirths (in the bardo state). With this practice, spirits are able to attain a higher level of rebirth. A bardo deliverance ceremony may be done for ancestors and other spirits.

Bodhisattva
An enlightened being who, out of compassion, forgoes nirvana to help save others.

Buddha-nature
The inherent nature of all sentient beings. All sentient beings have the potential to awaken their Buddha-nature and become buddhas.

Cheng Huang (City God)
A common Taoist deity who controls the spirits within a certain area (a town or city).

Devadatta
He was a Buddhist monk and a cousin of Shakyamuni Buddha. He was jealous of the Buddha and created a great schism amongst the Sangha (the Buddhist monastic community).

Dharani
Similar to mantra, however a dharani is longer.

Dharma
Often means the body of teachings expounded by the Buddha. The word is also used in Buddhist phenomenology as a term roughly equivalent to phenomenon, a basic unit of existence and/or experience.

Earth Deity
A Taoist deity who protects the area around a house or temple. He is said to be the Earth God of wealth and merit.

Enlightenment
The goal of all Buddhists. Only through enlightenment can we overcome samsara and enter nirvana.

Five Dhyani Buddhas
The five meditational Buddhas representing five qualities of Buddhas: Akshobhya (east), Amitabha (west), Amoghasiddhi (north), Ratnasambhava (south), and Vairocana (center).

Five Precepts
The most basic precepts of Buddhism: do not kill, do not steal, do not commit sexual misconduct, do not lie, and do not take intoxicants.

Four Noble Truths
The first and fundamental teaching of Shakyamuni Buddha. These truths are: the truth of suffering, the truth of the accumulation and origin of suffering, the truth of the cessation of suffering, and the truth of the path to the cessation of suffering.

Fourfold Refuge
Taking refuge in the Root Guru, the Buddha, the Dharma and the Sangha.

Guanyin Bodhisattva
Chinese name for Avalokitesvara Bodhisattva - the Bodhisattva of mercy and compassion.

Heart Mantra
When a buddha or bodhisattva reaches enlightenment, his enlightenment is mirrored through the frequency of his heart mantra. When one chants the heart mantra, a resonance is created which allows one to merge with that respective buddha or bodhisattva.

High King Avalokitesvara Sutra
The sutra includes the names of many buddhas and bodhisattvas of the three times and ten directions and has been in circulation since the Tang Dynasty. To chant the *High King Avalokitesvara Sutra* is equivalent to receiving blessings and empowerment from the buddhas and bodhisattvas of the ten directions.

Karma (Sanskrit, literally "action" or "deed")
The cycle of cause and effect. This concept is believed amongst the Buddhist, Hindu, Jain and Sikh traditions.

Ksitigarbha Bodhisattva (Sanskrit, literally "Womb of the Earth")
He has a vow to not reach buddhahood until all the hells are empty.

Ksitigarbha Sutra
The sutra recounts how Ksitigarbha became a bodhisattva, his great vows to rescue other sentient beings, and recounts his amazing filial piety in his past lifetimes. The sutra consists of thirteen chapters, divided into three sections.

Lineage Dharma Robe
A robe passed from master to disciple, representing the dharma teachings and lineage being transferred from master to disciple. Other objects may also be given: bowls, statues, prayer beads, etc.

Maha Prajna Paramita
The Perfection of Wisdom or Transcendent Wisdom to cross over from a state of suffering to a state of enlightenment.

Mahamayuri Vidyarajni (the Peacock Dharma Protector)
An emanation of Vairocana Buddha who has the power to create harmony, increase wealth, purify negative karma and protect practitioners from disasters.

Manjushri Bodhisattva
The Bodhisattva of wisdom and knowledge. His practices may be used to help gain wisdom, knowledge and eloquence. He is usually depicted as holding the *Prajnaparamita Sutra* and the Sword of Wisdom.

Mahasattva
A bodhisattva, who has reached the tenth level of bodhisattvahood, yet forgoes buddhahood in order to help all sentient beings.

Mani Pearl
It can fulfill all virtuous vows and attain all matters of excellence, commonly associated with Avalokitesvara Bodhisattva.

Mantra
Chants used for blessing, invocation of buddhas and bodhisattvas, offering, and many other uses.

Mantrayana
See Vajrayana.

Mara
Synonymous with devil. Mara manifests in the form of greed, anger, ignorance, jealousy, etc.

Marici Bodhisattva
Marici Bodhisattva has the power to make the practitioner invisible to danger (robbers, killers, etc).

Master Sakya Zhengkong
His Eminence Sakya Zhengkong Rinpoche transmitted the Sakya School's central teaching, Lamdre (The Fruit and its Path), and gave the Acharya Empowerment to Living Buddha Lian-sheng.

Mudra
Hand gestures used in Vajrayana Buddhism. There are different mudras for buddhas, bodhisattvas, dharma protectors, other deities, etc.

Nagas
Serpent-like spiritual beings living in caves, rivers and heavens.

Namo
Often placed in front of the name of an object of veneration, e.g., a buddha's name or a sutra, to express devotion to it.

Padma Family of Buddhas
The Padma Family of Buddhas refers to one of the Five Buddha Families, and the Padma Family is headed by Amitabha Buddha.

Padmakumara (Sanskrit, literally "Lotus Youth")
The sambhogakaya emanation of Living Buddha Lian-sheng, Grand Master Sheng-yen Lu.

Padmasambhava (Sanskrit, literally "Lotus Born")
Commonly known as the Second Buddha, after Shakyamuni Buddha. Padmasambhava was supremely accomplished in the esoteric arts and used his powers to defeat many demons and black magic practitioners in Tibet in the eighth century. He is the founder of the Nyingma tradition of Tibetan Buddhism. Padmasambhava is one of the principal deities of True Buddha School.

Prajna
The ultimate wisdom.

Pure Land School
One of the schools of Mahayana Buddhism in which the objective is to be reborn in Amitabha's Western Paradise.

Pure Lands of the Ten Directions
All of the various pure lands emanated by different buddhas.

Reverend Liaoming
Grand Master Lu met Reverend Liaoming (also known as Taoist Master Qingzhen) while he was residing on Jiji Mountain in Nantou County, Taiwan. Reverend Liaoming was a Vajrayana Master and the Fourteenth Generation Disciple of the Qingcheng Taoist School.

Rinpoche (Tibetan, literally "Precious One")
A title reserved for incarnate lamas and accomplished teachers.

Saha world
A universe where all are subjected to transmigration.

Samadhi (Sanskrit, literally "make firm")
Deep meditation.

Samsara (Sanskrit, literally "flow together")
The cycle of birth, death and rebirth (i.e. reincarnation).

Sangha
A Sanskrit word meaning community, assembly, association with a common goal. In Buddhism it refers to monks or nuns with a higher realization, though in modern times this term has been used to describe groups of Buddhist followers in general. They are responsible for teaching, spreading, translating, and maintaining the teachings of Buddha.

Sanskrit
The language of ancient India. Sanskrit was the language of the Hindu Priest Class and the Veda Scriptures. It was later adopted by Buddhists to record Buddhist scriptures.

Sanskrit syllable
Also called a "seed syllable." It is a single mantra sound.

Sentient beings
Broadly speaking, all beings with awareness who have not attained enlightenment and become buddhas. More narrowly, all living beings with awareness within the six realms of reincarnation.

Shakyamuni Buddha
Siddhartha Gautama was born in Lumbini, India (modern day Nepal) sometime between 563 BCE to 483 BCE. He later became known as Shakyamuni Buddha. "Shakya" was his clan name and "muni" means great sage, thus, "the great sage of the Shakya clan." At the age of twenty-nine he left his home, and achieved enlightenment under the Bodhi Tree at age thirty-five. He became the founder of Buddhism and spread the dharma to all beings.

Siddhartha
The name of the Buddha before he became known as Shakyamuni Buddha.

Siddhi (Sanskrit, literally "accomplishment" or "ability")
Refers to the accomplishments that come with spiritual practice. It can be the transcendental siddhi of attaining nirvana or it may refer to more mundane abilities like flying, clairvoyance, clairaudience, invisibility, etc.

Simhamukha
Also known as the Lion-Faced Dakini, she is the guru, the personal deity as well as the dharma protector of Padmasambhava.

Sixteenth Karmapa (August 14, 1924 – November 5, 1981)
Spiritual leader of the Karma Kagyu lineage of Tibetan Buddhism. The first incarnation of the Karmapa was in 1110 AD making this the longest line of Tibetan Tulkus. His Holiness the Sixteenth Gyalwa Karmapa bestowed the highest empowerment of the Five-Buddha Crown Empowerment on Living Buddha Lian-sheng.

Sixth Patriarch Huineng (638 AD – 713 AD)
A Chinese Zen master who is one of the most important figures in the entire tradition. He was the last lineage master to receive the dharma robe.

Skanda
Also known as Wei Tuo or Wei Tuo Bodhisattva. A guardian devoted to protecting Buddhist temples and practitioners.

Talisman
Metaphysical amulets infused with the power of the creator. They are drawn onto paper and then burned and eaten or carried by the person wishing to use the talisman's power. They may be used to help cure illnesses, offer protection from danger, create harmony in life, etc.

Tantrayana
See Vajrayana.

Tao (Dao)
Means "the path to the truth."

Taoism (Daoism)
Focuses on nature, the relationship between humanity and the cosmos, health and longevity, and wu wei (action through inaction), which is thought to produce harmony with the universe.

Tathagata
A Sanskrit word meaning one who has thus come; essentially, a synonym for Buddha.

Ten Good Deeds
From *The Avatamsaka Sutra*; the deeds are abstention from: killing, stealing, sexual misconduct, divisive speech, harsh speech, lying, irresponsible speech, greed, anger and foolishness.

Three lower realms
The realms of hell, hungry ghosts and animals.

Thubten Dargye
Vajra Acharya Thubten Dargye of the Gelug School gave the Highest Yoga Tantra empowerment to Living Buddha Lian-sheng, among many other empowerments.

True Buddha School
A Vajrayana sect founded by Living Buddha Lian-sheng, Sheng-yen Lu.

Tsongkhapa (1357-1419)
The founder of the Gelug Sect of Tibetan Buddhism. He set up strict rules for the Gelug Sect which contrasted with the much looser rules of the other three sects of Tibetan Buddhism at that time.

Twelve Links of Dependent Origination
These are: ignorance, karma, consciousness, name and form, the six senses, contact, sensation, desire, attachment, existence, life, and old age and death.

Usnisa Vijaya
She is known for her power to bless people with longevity and to relieve the suffering of samsara.

Vairocana Buddha
Also known as the Great Sun Buddha, he is one of the Five Dhyani Buddhas. He typically is depicted as white in color and holds either the Dharmachakra Mudra or the Supreme Wisdom Mudra.

Vajra (Sanskrit, literally "Diamond Scepter")
A ritual object which represents a thunderbolt or diamond which represent being indestructible.

Vajrayana
A major branch of Buddhism in which the guru teaches an accelerated path to enlightenment, using the techniques of chanting mantras, forming mudras and visualization.

Vasudhara (Sanskrit, literally "Stream of Gems")
She is the Buddhist Bodhisattva of wealth, prosperity, and abundance. She is often compared with the Hindu deity Lakshmi.

Vinaya School
A school of Buddhism which emphasizes discipline and precepts according to the Vinaya Pitaka.

Western Paradise
The Western Paradise, or Sukhavati, is the Pure Land of Amitabha Buddha. A pure land is a place where many Buddhists aspire to be reborn, where they may cultivate diligently until reaching enlightenment, without fear of falling back into the six realms of reincarnation.

Wrathful protectors
Also known as "vajra protectors" or "dharma protectors," wrathful deities are enlightened beings that take on wrathful forms and their function is to protect Buddhist practitioners.

Yamantaka (Sanskrit, literally "Conqueror of Death")
Commonly depicted with either a bull or buffalo head, he is the wrathful form of Manjushri Bodhisattva.

Zen (Chan) Buddhism
A sect of Buddhism that emphasizes using meditation and inner contemplation to reach enlightenment.

Zen Patriarch
This term is used to mean a major lineage master of Zen Buddhism. It is most often used to refer to the Zen or Chan Patriarchs in China, from Bodhidharma to Huineng.